THE UK
TOWER
AIR FRYER
Recipe Book

The UK Tower® Air Fryer Recipe Book by Emily Arthur

Copyright © 2022 Emily Arthur

All rights reserved. No portion of this book may be reproduced in any form without permission from the publisher.

ISBN: 9798353391494

Introduction

With inflation hitting homes , we've been seeking out ways to save around the house. In addition to being fast, convenient and easy to clean, it turns out an air fryer can also save you money each month since these machines typically use far less energy than a full-size oven. As an added bonus, an air fryer won't heat up the kitchen as much, so you won't have to blast the air conditioner as much while you're cooking.

This book will walk you through the process of cooking in your air fryer anything that you would cook in a regular oven, you can air fry everything. it includes: breakfasts, mains, snacks and desserts step by step in your Tower® Air Fryer (I promise you'll be amazed at how quickly it comes together).

AIR FRYER
BEGINNER GUIDE

How to Use an Air Fryer

Do you know how to use your air fryer? This beginner's guide will walk you through everything you need to know to get started with this multi functional kitchen appliance.

Contents

- What you can cook in an air fryer,
- what is an air fryer
- how to use an air fryer,
- safety precautions,
- cleaning your air fryer,
- and the best air fryer recipes.

1

WHAT YOU CAN COOK IN AN AIR FRYER

In an air fryer, you can cook almost anything! Proteins such as chicken, fish, or meat, as well as healthy vegetable side dishes, appetisers such as zucchini fries or chicken wings, and even desserts and baked goods. The air fryer is ideal for cooking foods that require a high level of crispiness or crunch, such as French fries, fried chicken, and baked potatoes with crispy skins. It's also cook meats like steak or chicken because it always results in juicy, flavorful results.

WHAT EXACTLY IS AN AIR FRYER?

An air fryer is a multi-purpose kitchen appliance that can be used to air fry, roast, bake, broil, crisp, dehydrate, and reheat foods.

Air fryers are classified into two types: basket air fryers and air fryer ovens.
Basket air fryers have a removable basket where you can place food.
Air fryer ovens resemble toaster ovens and have racks inside where you can place food.
Both types of air fryers function similarly.

How to Use an Air Fryer

1 You can use your air fryer to cook recipes that requires cooking in oven. Because the heat in an air fryer is more intense than in a standard oven, reduce the recommended temperature by 25F/5C to 50F/10C and the cooking time by about 20%. So, instead of cooking the food in the oven at 425F/232C for 60 minutes, air-fry it at 400F/205C for about 40 minutes.

2 To ensure even cooking, shake or flip the food halfway through. Give the basket a good shake about halfway through the cook time when cooking food in small pieces, such as Brussels sprouts or French fries, to promote even cooking and browning. Flip meat pieces over halfway through cooking time, such as meat or chicken.

3 To make foods crispy, dry them thoroughly. Pat food dry with a clean kitchen towel or paper towels before adding oil, seasonings, or placing it in the air fryer basket.

4 It is okay to remove the basket during the cooking cycle to check on the progress of your food.

IV

AIR FRYER SAFETY

1 An air fryer is designed for air frying rather than traditional oil frying, and the basket should never be filled with oil.

2 Cook in a well-ventilated area at all times. Allow enough space around the air fryer for the exhaust to circulate. Place it away from a wall.

3 After using the air fryer, keep your hands and countertops safe from the hot basket. When remove the hot basket from the air fryer, place it on a silicone trivet or pot holder/hot pad.

4 When not in use, unplug the air fryer.

5 Never use your air fryer near a heat source. Never set your air fryer on the stove.

6 Do not use perforated parchment paper at high temperatures unless it is covered with food. If there isn't enough food to weigh down the parchment paper, it will fly around and cover the food as the hot air circulates. This causes the food to cook unevenly. Also, if the parchment is flying around and comes into contact with the hot heating element, it may burn up.

7 Avoid overcrowding the air fryer basket. The food will not cook evenly, and the air will not circulate properly. When air frying, try to keep the food in a single layer.

V

CLEANING AIR FRYER

- Remember to clean your air fryer as you would any other kitchen appliance! After each use, air fryers should be lightly cleaned. Every few weeks, you should thoroughly clean your air fryer. It's important to clean the air fryer basket and drawer after each use.

- Unplug your air fryer before cleaning it.

- You can make cleanup even easier by using the following air fryer accessories:
  - Parchment paper
  - Silicone liner
  - Silicone basket
  - Aluminum foil

- Remember that proper maintenance will extend the life of your air fryer! A dirty air fryer can produce stale food and cause your air fryer to malfunction. Worse, it could result a kitchen fire.

- Warm, soapy water should be used to clean the removable components. Avoid using abrasives and instead use a soft sponge or cloth. If any of the parts have food stuck to them, soak them in hot water and dish detergent to loosen the food before cleaning.

- To remove food that has become stuck in the basket or grate, use a wooden skewer or toothpick.

- Use a damp cloth dipped in warm soapy water to clean the inside of the air fryer. The basket and drawer should be removed as well. Wipe away any grease or food debris from the heating element. Allow to dry before reassembling.

- Wipe the exterior with a damp cloth or sponge, then dry the appliance.

Index

Introduction I
What you can cook in an air fryer II
What exactly is an air fryer? III
How to Use an Air Fryer IV
Air Fryer Safety V
Cleaning Air Fryer VI

Breakfast

Reuben sandwich 1	Cheesy Baked Eggs 11
Grilled Cheese 1	Air Fryer Pop-Tarts 11
Stuffed zucchini boats with sausage 2	Crescent Breakfast Pockets 12
Scaloped potatoes 2	Egg Bites 12
Tuna patties 3	Hash brown bites breakfast bake 13
Baked egg cups with spinach & cheese . 3	Sausage Breakfast Casserole 13
Chocolate & wallnuts granola 4	Omelette frittata 14
Greek Frittata 4	Hot dog wraps 14
Baked Oats 5	Turkey melt 15
Hard Boiled Eggs 5	Zucchini Pizza Boats 15
Avocado Eggs 6	Breakfast Pizza 16
Dorito Cheese Bites 6	Breakfat Mac & Cheese 16
Breakfast Burritos 7	Brussels Sprouts Apple Nut Salad 17
Eggplant Parmesan Bites 7	Scotch Egg 17
Blueberry bread 8	Salami & Cheese Quesadilla 18
Croquettes with Egg & Asparagus 8	Avocado Toast 18
Salmon cakes 9	Baked Potato 19
Cheese & bean quesadillas 9	
Crispy Sauerkraut Fritters 10	
Roasted Oranges 10	

Fish

Healthy baked salmon 20
Air Fryer Salmon 20
Air Fried Shrimp 21
Prawn Fajitas 21

Fish & Chips	22
White fish with garlic & lemon	22
Swai fish	23
Shrimp cocktail	23
Salmon Fajitas	24
Parmesan Crusted Salmon	24
Crispy fish fillets	25
Mahi Mahi	25
Catfish	26
Tilapia	26
Shrimp and Vegetables	27
Tuna Melt	27
Fish tacos	28
Salmon bites	28
Cajun shrimp	29
Salmon Burgers	29
Honey Glazed Salmon	30
Honey Lime Shrimp	30
Coconut shrimp with orange dipping	31
Fried Shrimp	31
Bang Bang Shrimp	32
Crab Cakes	32
Salmon and Potatoes Bake	33
Shrimp Tacos	33

Poultry

Shepherd's Pie	34
Rosemary Ranch Chicken	34
Cheesy chicken sausage rolls	35
Baked Chicken Breast	35
Duck	36
Crispy skin whole chicken with herbs	36
Turkey burgers	37
"Shake 'N Bake" style chicken	37
Orange Chicken	38
Doritos crusted chicken strips	38
Herbed chicken breast	39
Chicken strips	39
Chicken parmesan	40
Stuffed Chicken Breasts	40
Air fryer turkey breast	41
Chicken burgers	41
BBQ chicken wings	42
Chinese chicken on a stick	42
lemon pepper chicken	43
BBQ Chicken Legs	43
Smoky Chicken	44
Teriyaki Chicken Thighs	44
Chicken Pesto	45
Sweet & Sour Chicken	45
Chicken kabobs	46
Chicken quesadilla	46
BBQ chicken kabobs	47
Honey garlic chicken wings	47
Cornish Hen	48
Chicken drumsticks	48
Chicken Street Tacos	49
Chicken Nuggets	49
Garlic parmesan chicken bites	50
Turkey meatballs	50
Kielbasa Veggie	51
Ramen Noodle Stir	51
Ranch Chicken and Veggies	52
Spicy Apricot Chicken	52
Honey Mustard Chicken Breasts	53
Roasted Chicken Sausage & Veggies	53
Chicken empanadas	54
Pizza Stuffed Chicken Thighs	54

Chicken Thighs 55

Meats

Beef & Cheese Quesadilla	56
Juicy Steak and Mushrooms Bites ..	56
Ground Beef Wellington	57
Stuffed Meat Loaf Slices	57
Papas Rellenas	58
Quick Tater Tots Bake	58
Beef Wellington Wontons	59
Mongolian Beef	59
Korean BBQ Beef	60
Kofta kebabs	60
Empanadas	61
Cheese stuffed meatballs	61
Steak bites	62
Flank steak	62
Sausage Balls	63
Corned beef	63
Meatloaf	64
Rosemary garlic lamb chops	64
Steak	65
Beef Roast	65
Taco bell dorito crunch wrap	66
Crescent Roll Meatballs	66
Lasagna	67
Pigs in a Blanket	67
Crustless Quiche	68
Beef Jerky	68
Pepperoni Stromboli	69
Stuffed Peppers	69
Swedish Meatballs	70

Vegetables

Spiced Black Bean Tacos	71
Roasted Fall Vegetables	71
Squash Soup	72
Potato wedges	72
Fried green tomatoes	73
Plantains	73
Kale Chips	74
Falafel	74
Air Fryer Apples	75
Eggplant	75
Cajun Scallops	76
Roasted Okra	76
Green Beans	77
Ratatouille Gnocchi	77
Smashed Potatoes	78
Air Fryer Pineapple	78
Garlic mushrooms	79
Roasted Potatoes	79
Butternut squash	80
Roasted brussels sprouts	80
Acorn squash	81
Asparagus	81
Garlic Carrots	82
Sweet potato fries	82
Corn on the cob	83
Green Bean Casserole	83
Cauliflower with garlic	84

Snacks & Sides

Roasted Parmesan Tomatoes 85
Crispy Onion 85
Vegetarian Quesadilla 86
Mozzarella Sticks 86
Gingerbread Bites 87
Pasta chips 87
Egg rolls 88
Toasted ravioli 88
Cheese wontons 89
Chin chin 89
Jalapeño Poppers 90
Stuffed Peppers 90
Tortilla Chips 91
Fried Rice 91
Sausage Crescent Cheese Balls 92
Onion rings 92
Eggplant Parmesan 93
Jicama fries 93
Fetta Nuggets 94
Crispy tofu bites 94
Jojo potato wedges 95
Fried Pickles 95
Spinach dip 96
Cheesy mushroom 96
Sweet potato rolls 97
Garlic Bread 97
Crispy breaded broccoli bites 98
Turnips 98
Arancini 99
Courgette fries 99
Croutons 100

Pizza

Margherita Pizza 101
Eggplant pizza 101
Breakfast Pizzas with English Muffins ... 102
Zucchini Pizza Bites 102
Pizza Bombs 103
Pizza Pockets 103
Pizza Rolls 104
Pepperoni pizza egg rolls 104
Biscuit mini pizzas 105

Desserts

Pizookie 106
Peanut Butter and Jelly 106
Air Fryer Biscuits 107
Blueberry muffins 107
Cannoli 108
Banana Muffins 108
Chocolate Banana Muffins 109
Shortbread cookies 109
Scotch pancakes 110
Lemonade scones 110
Apple Hand Pies 111
Peanut Butter Cookies 111
Blueberry Hand Pies 112
Jelly donuts 112
Caramelized bananas 113
Buttermilk Drop Biscuits 113

Air Fried Oreos	**114**
Sweet Apples	**114**
Creamed Corn Casserole	**115**
Pumpkin Pie	**115**
Corn bread	**116**
Peach Crisp	**116**
Mini lemon pies	**117**
Peanut butter oat cookies	**117**
Chocolate Chip Cookies	**118**
Eggy bread	**118**
Air Fried Churros	**119**
Apple Crumble	**119**
Apple Fritters	**120**
Chocolate fudge brownies	**120**
Strawberry Rhubarb Crumbles	**121**
Apple Pie Filo Pastries	**121**
Chocolate Cupcakes	**122**
Banana Bundt Cake	**122**
Cinnamon Rolls	**123**
Strawberry shortcake	**123**
Banana Souffle	**124**
Banana Bread	**124**
Blueberry Scones	**125**
Air Fryer Donuts	**125**
Hand Pies	**126**
Pumpkin Chocolate Chip Muffins	**126**
Lemon Baked Donuts	**127**
Nutella French Toast Roll Up	**127**
Creme Brulee	**128**
Sweet potato pie	**128**

REUBEN SANDWICH

Serving Size	Prep Time	Cooking time	Total Time
4 Servings	12 Minutes	6 Minutes	16 Minutes

Ingredients

- 8 slices bread
- 4 slices Swiss cheese
- 500g corned beef sliced
- 8 tbsp sauerkraut, (drained)
- 120g Thousand Island dressing
- Melted butter

Directions

1. Preheat air fryer to 390°F/200°C
2. spread the Thousand Island dressing on bread slices. Divide corned beef evenly among 4 pieces of bread, then top with sauerkraut and a slice of cheese. Then top the sandwiches with the 4 remaining slices of bread. Use a toothpick to hold the sandwiches together.
3. Put the sandwiches in air fryer basket, and brush the top with melted butter.
4. Air fry 4 minutes, then flip, and brush butter on the tops. Air fry for another 3 minutes.

Calories: 562kcal | Carbohydrates: 35g | Protein: 28g | Fat: 35g | Fiber: 3g | Sugar: 9g

GRILLED CHEESE

Serving Size	Prep Time	Cooking time	Total Time
2 Servings	5 Minutes	3 Minutes	8 Minutes

Ingredients

- 4 slices bread
- 4 slices cheese
- 2 tbsp butter softened (or mayo)

Directions

1. Preheat air fryer to 390°F/200°C
2. Butter outside of bread, placing 2 slices of cheese in the middle of each sandwich.
3. Air fry for 3 minutes on each side.

477kcal, Fat: 25g, Carbohydrates: 28g, Protein:15g

STUFFED ZUCCHINI BOATS WITH SAUSAGE

Serving Size	Prep Time	Cooking time	Total Time
4 Servings	5 Minutes	15 Minutes	20 Minutes

Ingredients

- 2 medium zucchini, (halved & cored)
- 250g uncooked sausage meat
- 60g breadcrumbs
- 60g grated cheese
- 1/2 red bell pepper, (chopped)
- Cooking spray

Directions

1. Spray zucchini with cooking spray.
2. Stuff the zucchini center with sausage. Top with breadcrumbs, bell pepper and cheese. Spray with cooking spray.
3. Put zucchini in the air fryer basket.
4. Air fry at 355°F/180°C for 14 minutes.
5. Serve with your favorite sauce.

calories: 285kcal, carbohydrates: 9g, protein: 16g, fat: 21g, fiber: 1g, sugar: 3g

SCALLOPED POTATOES

Serving Size	Prep Time	Cooking time	Total Time
4 Servings	15 Minutes	35 Minutes	55 Minutes

Ingredients

- 500g potatoes, (cut into thin slices)
- 3 tbsp oil
- 200ml heavy cream
- 1/4 tsp garlic powder
- 60g shredded cheddar cheese
- Salt & pepper to taste
- Cooking spray

Directions

1. In a large mixing bowl, add potato slices and oil. Mix until potatoes fully coated with oil.
2. Spray 7-inch/18cm cake pan with cooking spray. Add the potato slices in stack into the prepared cake pan. Put the pan in the air fryer basket.
3. Air Fry at 355°F/180°C for 18 minutes.
4. In a medium mixing bowl, add heavy cream, garlic powder and season with salt & pepper. Mix until combined.
5. After 18 minutes, pour the cream over the potatoes. Air fry again at 300°F/150°C for 18 minutes.
6. Sprinkle shredded cheddar cheese over the potatoes. Air fry for additional 2 minutes.
7. Remove from air fryer. Allow to cool 10 minutes before serving.

calories: 378kcal, carbohydrates: 30g, protein: 9g, fat: 25g, fiber: 2g, sugar: 1g.

TUNA PATTIES

Serving Size	Prep Time	Cooking time	Total Time
10 Servings	15 Minutes	10 Minutes	25 Minutes

Ingredients

- 500g canned albacore tuna or diced fresh tuna
- 3 large eggs
- zest of 1 lemon
- 1 tbsp lemon juice
- 60g breadcrumbs
- 3 tbsp grated Parmesan cheese
- 1 stalk celery, (finely chopped)
- 3 tbsp minced onion
- 1/2 tsp garlic powder
- 1/2 tsp dried oregano
- Salt & pepper to taste

Directions

1. In a medium mixing bowl, add eggs, lemon zest, lemon juice, breadcrumbs, Parmesan cheese, celery, onion, garlic powder, dried oregano, season with salt & pepper. Mix until combined. Add in the tuna, gently mix until just combined.
2. Divide the mixture into 10 balls. Shape into patties about 1cm thick. Chill them for at about 1 hour or until firm.
3. Spray air fryer basket with cooking spray. Add tuna patties in the basket and spray the top with cooking spray.
4. Air Fry 350°F/180°C, 10 minutes, flipping & spraying with cooking spray halfway through cooking time.
5. Serve with your favorite sauce.

calories: 85kcal, carbohydrates: 1g, protein: 13g, fat: 3g, fiber: 1g, sugar: 1g.

BAKED EGG CUPS WITH SPINACH & CHEESE

Serving Size	Prep Time	Cooking time	Total Time
1 Servings	3 Minutes	12 Minutes	15 Minutes

Ingredients

- 1 large egg
- 1 tbsp milk
- 1 tbsp frozen or fresh spinach
- 2 tsp grated cheese
- Salt & pepper to taste
- Cooking Spray

Directions

1. Spray a ramekin with cooking spray.
2. Add all ingredients in the ramekin. Mix until all combined.
3. Air Fry at 325°F/165°C. for 12 minutes.

calories: 115kcal, carbohydrates: 1g, protein: 10g, fat: 7g, sugar: 1g.

CHOCOLATE & WALLNUTS GRANOLA

Serving Size	Prep Time	Cooking time	Total Time
8 Servings	5 Minutes	10 Minutes	15 Minutes

Ingredients

- 275g Rolled Oats
- 75g Almonds (Whole)
- 75g raisins or dried fruits
- 50g pumpkin seeds
- 25g Flaked coconut shavings
- 100g Dark Chocolate Chips
- 90g Chocolate Protein Powder
- 100ml Coconut oil (Melted)
- 2 tsp. Vanilla extract
- 1 tsp. Peanut butter
- 120ml Maple syrup

Directions

1. In a large bowl, add oats, hazelnuts & chocolate protein powder, mix.
2. In a smaller bowl whisk melted coconut oil, maple syrup, peanut butter and vanilla. pour over hazelnut, oats and protein powder mixture. Stir until combined.
3. Pour granola mixture directly into air fryer basket.
4. Air fry 340°F/170°C for 6 minutes, use a fork to separate and mix granola within air fryer basket. Cook for more 3 minutes and break up the granola with a fork. Finally air fry for another 3 minutes.
5. Remove granola from air fryer by pouring over parchment paper lined oven tray. Once cooled sprinkle chocolate chips and coconut flakes over. Serve straight away with milk or yogurt or smoothie bowl.
6. Store the remaining granola in an air tight jar, will keep for 2-3 weeks.

Calories: 393kcal | Carbohydrates: 43g | Protein: 22g | Fat: 16g | Fiber: 6g | Sugar: 10g

GREEK FRITTATA

Serving Size	Prep Time	Cooking time	Total Time
2 Serving	10 Minutes	20 Minutes	30 Minutes

Ingredients

- cooking spray
- 4 large eggs
- 3 tbsp heavy whipping cream
- handful chopped spinach leaves
- 75g feta cheese
- 80g cherry tomatoes, halved
- 60g diced red onion
- 1 tsp dried oregano
- salt & pepper to taste

Directions

1. Preheat an air fryer to 350°F/176°C. Spray a 6-inch/15cm cake pan with cooking spray.
2. Whisk eggs and cream in a bowl. Add spinach, feta cheese, cherry tomatoes, onion, oregano, salt, and pepper. Mix well combined. Pour into prepared cake pan and cover with foil.
3. Air fry for 12 minutes. Remove foil and air fry for 6 minutes longer.

Calories: 415kcal | Carbohydrates: 11g | Protein: 24g | Fat: 131g | Sodium: 826mg | Fiber: 1g | Sugar: 3g

BAKED OATS

Serving Size	Prep Time	Cooking time	Total Time
2 Servings	2 Minutes	15 Minutes	17 Minutes

Ingredients

- ½ large Banana
- 40g rolled oats
- 1 tbsp maple syrup
- 1 tsp vanilla extract
- ½ tsp baking powder
- 1 Large Egg
- 60g milk of choice
- ½ tsp ground cinnamon or nutmeg
- blueberries or your favorite fruits

Directions

1. Grease 2 ramekins and set aside. Add all ingredients into the blender. Blend till smooth.
2. Add oats mixture to ramekins and top with fruits.
3. Bake in air fryer at 330°F / 165°C for 15 mins.
4. Remove from air fryer add your favorite toppings.

Calories: 190kcal | Carbohydrates: 30g | Protein: 7g | Fat: 4g | Sodium: 53mg | Fiber: 3g | Sugar: 12g

HARD BOILED EGGS

Serving Size	Prep Time	Cooking time	Total Time
9 Eggs	5 Minutes	15 Minutes	25 Minutes

Ingredients

- 9 large eggs
- salt and pepper to taste

Directions

1. Preheat the air fryer to 270°F/135°C.
2. Place eggs in air fryer basket and cook for 15 minutes.
3. prepare ice bath by filling a bowl with water and ice.
4. When eggs are done cooking, place them into ice bath to cool.
5. Peel and eat immediately or cool completely in refrigerator for up to 5-6 days.

Calories: 63kcal | Carbohydrates: 1g | Protein: 6g | Fat: 4g | Sodium: 62mg | Fiber: 1g | Sugar: 1g

AVOCADO EGGS

Serving Size	Prep Time	Cooking time	Total Time
4 Servings	12 Minutes	12 Minutes	17 Minutes

Ingredients

- 2 avocados
- 4 eggs
- 2-4 slices bread

Directions

1. Cut the avocados in half lengthwise. Remove the pit. Carve out some of the avocado flesh.
2. Place parchment paper in the air fryer basket.
3. Place the avocados on top of parchment paper. Place bread slices around the avocados. Crack 1 egg into the cavity of each avocado half. Season with salt and pepper.
4. you can add any additional toppings paprika or parmesan cheese.
5. Cook at 370°F/187°C for 12 minutes or until eggs are done.
6. Remove from the air fryer basket and serve.

Calories: 262kcal | Carbohydrates: 16g | Protein: 9g | Fat: 20g | Sodium: 136mg | Fiber: 7g | Sugar: 2g

DORITO CHEESE BITES

Serving Size	Prep Time	Cooking time	Total Time
2 Servings	10 Minutes	6 Minutes	16 Minutes

Ingredients

- 90g cup flour divided
- 1 egg whisked
- 4-8 Babybel cheeses frozen
- 3 handfuls of Doritos

Directions

1. Prepare 3 shallow bowls. One 60g flour. Second, egg. Third, crushed Doritos with 90g flour, mixed together.
2. pray the air fryer basket with cooking spray.
3. Unwrap the cheese bites. Cover each cheese bite in the flour, egg wash, then Doritos mixture. Cover it in egg wash again, then in Dorito mixture again.
4. Press down on cheese. Place cheese inside and lightly spray with cooking spray.
5. Cook at 370°F/188°C for 3 minutes. Flip, and cook for an additional 3 minutes.

Calories: 213kcal | Carbohydrates: 36g | Protein: 8g | Fat: 3g | Sodium: 48mg | Fiber: 1g | Sugar: 1g

BREAKFAST BURRITOS

Serving Size	Prep Time	Cooking time	Total Time
6 Servings	15 Minutes	5 Minutes	20 Minutes

Ingredients

- 6 medium flour tortillas
- 6 scrambled eggs
- ½ bell pepper – minced

<u>*Additions*</u>

- grape tomatoes, sliced
- 1 small onion, diced
- 120 g grated cheddar cheese
- 1 medium bell pepper, diced
- cooked sausage or bacon
- or you can add your favorite additions

Directions

1. Combine scrambled eggs, bell pepper, bacon bits, and cheese in a large bowl. Stir to combine.
2. Spoon about a ½ cup of the mixture into the center of a flour tortilla.
3. Fold in the additions & then roll.
4. Place the filled burritos into the air fryer basket & spray with cooking spray.
5. Cook at 330°F/165°C. for 5 minutes until hot and slightly crispy.

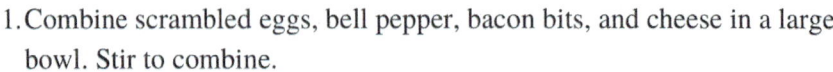

EGGPLANT PARMESAN BITES

Serving Size	Prep Time	Cooking time	Total Time
5 Servings	15 Minutes	15 Minutes	30 Minutes

Ingredients

- 1 large eggplant
- ¼ tsp sea salt
- 450g panko crumbs
- 50g parmesan cheese grated
- 1 tbsp Italian seasoning
- 2 tsp garlic powder
- 1 tsp salt
- 1 pinch red pepper flakes
- 2 eggs

Directions

1. Cut the eggplant into 1 inch/2.5cm cubes and sprinkle with a ¼ tsp salt. set aside.
2. Combine panko crumbs with parmesan cheese, Italian seasoning, garlic powder, salt, and red pepper flakes into a shallow bowl. Whisk eggs in another shallow bowl.
3. Dip eggplant cubes into egg wash then breading mixture.
4. Place cubes in greased air fryer basket. Spray the tops of cubes with cooking spray and cook at 380°F/190°C for 12 minutes, flipping halfway point.
5. Remove from the air fryer and enjoy with favorite sauce.

Calories: 222kcal | Carbohydrates: 27g | Protein: 4g | Fat: 13g | Sodium: 140mg | Fiber: 5g | Sugar: 17g

BLUEBERRY BREAD

Serving Size	Prep Time	Cooking time	Total Time
2 Servings	5 Minutes	30 Minutes	35 Minutes

Ingredients

- 240g milk
- 340g pancake mix
- 60g protein powder
- 3 eggs
- 225g frozen blueberries

Directions

1. Mix all ingredients together until combined. The mixture will be thick.
2. Place into a loaf pan and air fry at 350°F/175°C for 30 minutes.
3. To check to see if the bread is done, insert a toothpick, if the bread is done, it should come out clean.

Calories: 140kcal | Carbohydrates: 18g | Protein: 5g | Fat: 5g | Sodium: 33mg | Fiber: 17g | Sugar: 2g

CROQUETTES WITH EGG & ASPARAGUS

Serving Size	Prep Time	Cooking time	Total Time
6 Serving	30 Minutes	15 Minutes	45 Minutes

Ingredients

- 3 tbsps butter
- 3 tbsps all-purpose flour
- 200ml milk
- 6 hard-boiled large eggs, chopped
- 65g chopped fresh asparagus
- 50g chopped green onions
- 50g shredded cheddar cheese
- 1 tbsp minced fresh tarragon
- salt & pepper to taste
- 80g panko bread crumbs
- 3 large eggs, beaten

Directions

1. In a large saucepan over medium heat, melt butter. Stir in flour until smooth; cook and stir for 2 minutes until browned. Gradually whisk in milk; cook and stir until thickened. Stir in hard-boiled eggs, asparagus, green onions, cheese, tarragon, salt and pepper. Refrigerate at least 2 hours.
2. Preheat air fryer to 350°F/175°C. Shape 1/4 cup egg mixture into twelve 3-in/7.5cm long ovals. Place bread crumbs and eggs in separate shallow bowls. Roll logs in crumbs to coat, then dip in egg and roll again in crumbs.
3. In batches, place croquettes in a single layer on greased tray in air-fryer basket; spray with cooking spray. Cook for 10 minutes until golden brown. Turn; spray with cooking spray. Cook for 4 minutes.

Calories: 294kcal | Carbohydrates: 17g | Protein: 3g | Fat: 17g | Sodium: 348mg | Fiber: 1g | Sugar: 3g

SALMON CAKES

Serving Size	Prep Time	Cooking time	Total Time
4 Servings	12 Minutes	8 Minutes	20 Minutes

Ingredients

- 420 tinned salmon, (boneless)
- 2 eggs
- 1 tbsp mayonnaise
- ½ bell pepper red
- ½ cup breadcrumbs
- ½ tsp garlic powder
- 2 tbsp fresh parsley, (chopped)
- Salt & pepper to taste
- Cooking spray

Directions

1. Preheat the air fryer to 390°F/200°C.
2. In a large mixing bowl, add salmon, breadcrumbs, eggs, and all the seasonings. Mix until combined.
3. Divide the salmon into 60g patties.
4. Form the salmon patties to be no larger than 2.5cm thick.
5. Add the salmon patties to the air fryer basket. Spray the patties with cooking spray and cook for 8 minutes. Then flip the patties, spray with cooking spray, and cook for another 2 minutes.
6. Serve with your favorite dipping sauce.

Calories: 273kcal, Carbohydrates: 11g, Protein: 26g, Fat: 13g, Fiber: 1g, Sugar: 2g.

CHEESE & BEAN QUESADILLAS

Serving Size	Prep Time	Cooking time	Total Time
4 Servings	15 Minutes	5 Minutes	20 Minutes

Ingredients

- 1/2 tbsp. olive oil
- 4 spring onions, (chopped)
- 1 red pepper, (chopped)
- 1 400g tin black beans, (rinsed & drained)
- 200g corn kernels
- 2 tbsp. tomato puree
- 4 tbsp. water
- 1/2 tsp. ground cumin
- 1/2 tsp. paprika
- Salt & pepper to taste
- 4 tortillas
- 120g grated cheddar cheese

Directions

1. In a large pan over medium heat. Heat oil, add the spring onion and pepper, fry for 2 min. Add beans, tomato puree, corn, water, cumin, paprika and season with salt & pepper. Cooking for 3 min.
2. Divide the bean mixture over 4 tortillas, spread it only on half of each tortilla, sprinkle the cheese over the beans
3. Fold over the other half of the tortillas, gently pressing down. Place them in the air fryer basket.
4. Air fry at 350°F/180°C. for 3 minutes each side.
5. Serve with salsa.

380kcal, Fat: 14g, Carbohydrates: 50g, Protein:20g

CRISPY SAUERKRAUT FRITTERS

Serving Size	Prep Time	Cooking time	Total Time
4 Servings	60 Minutes	11 Minutes	5H 11 Minutes

Ingredients

Fritter
- 450g sauerkraut, drained
- 1 large smoked sausage, cut into small pieces
- 170g thick-cut bacon, cut into small pieces
- 2 tbsp mustard
- 85g cheese grated
- 3 large eggs lightly beaten
- 60g Panko crumbs

Fritter Breading
- 190g flour
- salt & pepper to taste
- 2 large eggs beaten
- 90 g Panko crumbs

Directions

1. in skillet over medium heat. add bacon and sausage and cook for 7 minutes. Remove from heat and allow to cool. add bacon and sausage to drained sauerkraut. Add mustard, Panko crumbs, and grated cheese and mix.
2. Stir in eggs and mix. Cover mixture and set in refrigerator for at least three hours. use a 2-tbsp cookie scoop to form into balls. Set balls on a plate and cover. Refrigerate at least one hour.
3. Prepare 3 bowls, Bowl 1: Flour, salt, and pepper. Stir . Bowl 2: Beaten eggs. Bowl 3: Panko crumbs
4. Remove fritter from refrigerator. Roll each fritter in flour mixture, then dip in beaten egg, and roll in Panko crumbs.
5. Transfer fritter in air fryer basket. Cook at 360°F /180°C for 11 minutes. flipping halfway through cooking process.
6. Serve with Sauce

Calories: 123kcal | Carbohydrates: 12g | Protein: 5g | Fat: 6g | Sodium: 390mg | Fiber: 1g | Sugar: 1g

ROASTED ORANGES

Serving Size	Prep Time	Cooking time	Total Time
4 Serving	1 Minutes	4 Minutes	5 Minutes

Ingredients

- 2 oranges
- 2 tsp honey
- 1 tsp cinnamon

Directions

1. Slice oranges in half.
2. Preheat an air fryer to 395°F/200°C .
3. Place the oranges in air fryer, and drizzle cinnamon and honey on top.
4. Air fry oranges for 6 minutes until golden on top. Serve while still warm

Calories: 43kcal | Carbohydrates: 11g | Protein: 1g | Fat: 1g | Sodium: 1mg | Fiber: 2g | Sugar: 9g

CHEESY BAKED EGGS

Serving Size	Prep Time	Cooking time	Total Time
2 Servings	4 Minutes	16 Minutes	20 Minutes

Ingredients

- 4 large Eggs
- 60g Smoked gouda, chopped
- Everything bagel seasoning
- salt & pepper to taste

Directions

1. Spray the inside of 2 ramekin with cooking spray. Add 2 eggs to each ramekin, then add 30g gouda to each. Salt and pepper to taste. Sprinkle seasoning on top of each ramekin. Stir.
2. Place each ramekin into the air fryer basket. Cook at 400°F/205°C for 16 minutes, or until eggs are cooked through. Serve.

Calories: 240kcal | Carbohydrates: 1g | Protein: 12g | Fat: 16g

AIR FRYER POP-TARTS

Serving Size	Prep Time	Cooking time	Total Time
4 Serving	10 Minutes	7 Minutes	19 Minutes

Ingredients

- Pre-Made Pie Crust
- Grape Jelly
- Vanilla Icing
- Sprinkles
- 1 Egg

Directions

1. Roll out the pie crust and cut out 3 inch/7.5cm rectangles.
2. Place a tsp of grape jelly in the center of half of rectangles.
3. Place a rectangle on top of the jelly rectangles & press edges together with a fork. Egg wash each rectangle.
4. Place in air fryer, cook at at 370°F/190°C for 8 minutes.
5. Remove from air fryer and smother in icing.
6. Sprinkle away!

Calories: 219kcal | Carbohydrates: 26g | Protein: 3g | Fat: 11g | Sodium: 174mg | Fiber: 0g | Sugar: 9g

CRESCENT BREAKFAST POCKETS

Serving Size	Prep Time	Cooking time	Total Time
8 Servings	10 Minutes	10 Minutes	20 Minutes

Ingredients

- 240g packages refrigerated crescent rolls
- 240g chicken sausage
- 1 tbsp butter
- 4 large eggs
- salt & pepper to taste
- 45g shredded Cheddar cheese

Directions

1. Preheat air fryer to 350°F/176°C.
2. Unroll crescent dough and separate into 16 triangles. Slice sausage into coin-sized pieces.
3. Melt butter in a large skillet over medium-high heat. Add eggs and sausage pieces and season with salt & pepper. Cook for 2 minutes, stirring, until cooked.
4. Place about 2 tbsp of filling and Cheddar cheese onto 8 of crescent triangles. Place remaining crescents on top of filling. Pinch to seal triangle pockets.
5. Cook in air fryer for 6 minutes until golden brown. Serve immediately.

Calories: 363kcal | Carbohydrates: 23g | Protein: 22g | Fat: 23g | Sugar: 5g

EGG BITES

Serving Size	Prep Time	Cooking time	Total Time
7 Servings	5 Minutes	12 Minutes	17 Minutes

Ingredients

- 7 Whole Eggs
- 60g Half and Half
- 1 Bell Pepper Chopped
- 40g Onion Chopped
- Chopped Bacon
- Salt & Pepper to Taste
- Shredded Sharp Cheddar Cheese
- Silicone Egg Mold

Directions

1. In bowl, beat the with the half and half. Mix in the bell pepper, onion, and bacon. Add salt and pepper.
2. Pour egg mixture evenly into a silicone mold, stopping just below the top of the mold. Top with cheese, before cooking.
3. Place the mold carefully into air fryer basket. Cook at 390°F/200°C for 12 minutes.
4. Once done, let sit for 3 minutes to cool.
5. Carefully using the mitts remove the basket and flip the mold out of the basket onto a cutting board or tray.
6. Carefully release the egg bites from the mold and serve. If any get stuck use a spoon to release.

calories: 165kcal, carbohydrates: 3g, protein: 15g, fat: 10g, fiber: 1g, sugar: 2g | Sodium: 425mg.

HASH BROWN BITES BREAKFAST BAKE

Serving Size	Prep Time	Cooking time	Total Time
5 Servings	10 Minutes	10 Minutes	25 Minutes

Ingredients

- 24 hash brown bites, (250g)
- 120g sausage, (sliced)
- 3 large eggs
- 2 tbsp milk
- 30g cheese
- 2 green onions, (chopped)
- Cooking spray
- Salt & pepper to taste

Directions

1. Spray 20cm baking pan with cooking spray. Spread hash brown bites in an even layer in pan and spray with cooking spray.
2. Air fry 380°F/195°C for 7 minutes.
3. Add sausage pieces to hash brown bites, nestling it in-between the hash brown bites. Air fry for 3 minutes.
4. In a medium bowl, add eggs, milk, cheese, green onions, season with salt & pepper. whisk until combined.
5. Pour egg mixture into pan with hash brown bites and sausage. Spread egg mixture to coat in-between hash brown bites & sauage.
6. Air fry 320°F/160°C for 10 minutes.
7. Remove from air fryer. Allow to cool slightly and serve.

calories: 424kcal, carbohydrates: 32g, protein: 17g, fat: 26g, fiber: 2g, sugar: 2g

SAUSAGE BREAKFAST CASSEROLE

Serving Size	Prep Time	Cooking time	Total Time
6 Servings	15 Minutes	10 Minutes	25 Minutes

Ingredients

- 500g hash browns
- 500g ground breakfast sausage
- 1 green bell pepper, (chopped)
- 1 red bell pepper, (chopped)
- 1 yellow bell pepper, (chopped)
- 1 onion, (chopped)
- 4 eggs
- Salt & pepper to taste

Directions

1. Line the bottom of air fryer basket with parchment paper.
2. Put the hash browns on the bottom. Then top with the uncooked sausage. Sprinkle the peppers and onion on top.
3. Air fry at 355°F/180°C for 10 minutes.
4. When time is up, open air fryer & mix up the casserole a bit. Crack eggs in a bowl, whisk then pour right on top of the casserole.
5. Air fry at 355°F/180°C for another 10 minutes.
6. Remove from air fryer. Serve.

calories: 517kcal, carbohydrates: 27g, protein: 21g, fat: 30g, fiber: 3g, sugar: 4g

13

OMELETTE FRITTATA

Serving Size	Prep Time	Cooking time	Total Time
2 Servings	10 Minutes	10 Minutes	20 Minutes

Ingredients

- 4 Eggs
- 2 tbsp Milk
- 1 Tomato, (chopped)
- 2 sprig Spring onions, (chopped)
- ½ tsp paprika
- ½ tsp garlic powder
- 50g Chopped Cooked Meat- chicken, beef, sausage
- Salt & pepper to taste
- Cooking spray

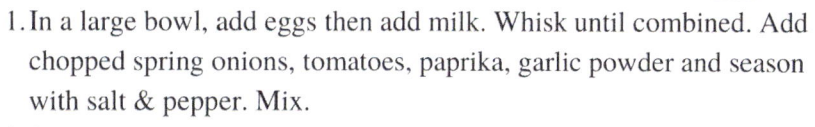

Directions

1. In a large bowl, add eggs then add milk. Whisk until combined. Add chopped spring onions, tomatoes, paprika, garlic powder and season with salt & pepper. Mix.
2. Spray a pan with cooking spray. Pour egg mixture into the baking pan. top with cheese.
3. Put the pan in air fryer basket. Air fry at 185°F/140°C for 11 minutes.
4. Remove from air fryer, serve.

Calories: 154kcal | Carbohydrates: 6g | Protein: 12g | Fat: 9g | Fiber: 2g | Sugar: 3g

HOT DOG WRAPS

Serving Size	Prep Time	Cooking time	Total Time
5 Servings	5 Minutes	8 Minutes	15 Minutes

Ingredients

- 5 hot dogs
- 5 slices of Bread
- 2 tbsp Butter
- 5 Slices of cheese

Directions

1. If you're using a thick bread type, flatten each slice of bread with a rolling pin and set aside.
2. Put a slice of cheese in middle of each bread. Put a hot dog at the edge of each bread slice. Roll it up.
3. Brush butter on the top of the bread wrapping the hot dogs.
4. Put in the air fryer basket.
5. Air fry at 390°F/200°C for 8 mins, flipping halfway through cooking time.

Calories: 366kcal | Carbohydrates: 7g | Protein: 14g | Fat: 31g | Fiber: 0.2g | Sugar: 2g

TURKEY MELT

Serving Size	Prep Time	Cooking time	Total Time
1 Servings	5 Minutes	8 Minutes	15 Minutes

Ingredients

- 2 slices bread
- Turkey slices
- 1 tbsp butter
- Sun dried tomato
- Swiss or cheddar cheese slices

Directions

1. Put cheese, sun dried tomato and turkey slices in between bread. Brush outside of bread with butter. Secure with toothpicks.
2. Put sandwich in air fryer basket.
3. Air Fry at 365°F/185°C for 5 minutes to melt the cheese.
4. Flip and air fry another 3 minutes.

calories: 592kcal, carbohydrates: 30g, protein: 47g, fat: 31g, fiber: 2g, sugar: 4g

ZUCCHINI PIZZA BOATS

Serving Size	Prep Time	Cooking time	Total Time
4 Servings	5 Minutes	8 Minutes	13 Minutes

Ingredients

- 2 Zucchini, (cut lengthwise)
- 60g Pizza Sauce
- Mini Pepperoni
- Shredded Mozzarella Cheese
- sliced green olives
- sliced cherry tomato
- Olive Oil Spray

Directions

1. Core the Zucchini middle out with a spoon. Spray the courgette with cooking spray.
2. Brush the Zucchini with pizza sauce, top with pepperoni, olives, tomato and cheese. Put them in the air fryer basket. Coat them with cooking spray.
3. Air fry at 355°F/180°C for 8 minutes. Repeat if necessary for the additional Zucchini.

61kcal Fat: 4g, Carbohydrates: 3g, Protein:3g

BREAKFAST PIZZA

Serving Size	Prep Time	Cooking time	Total Time
6 Servings	15 Minutes	15 Minutes	30 Minutes

Ingredients

For the Pizza Dough
- 120g all purpose flour
- 1 tbsp. granulated sugar
- 1 tsp baking powder
- 1/8 tsp salt
- 150g Greek yogurt
- 2 egg white

For the Toppings
- 4 slices Beef bacon, cut into thin strips
- 4 large eggs, beaten
- 60g cream cheese, room temp
- 60g freshly shredded cheese

Directions

1. In a large mixing bowl, add flour, sugar, baking powder, and salt. Mix everything together, add yogurt and mix until form a ball of dough.
2. Use a rolling pin to stretch the pizza dough out into a 20cm round. Brush the top with egg whites.
3. Spray air fryer basket with cooking spray, add pizza to the basket.
4. Air fry at 370°F/190°C for 10 mins, then flip and air fry for more 3 mins.
5. In a skillet over medium-high heat. Add bacon strips and cook. Once cooked, remove skillet from heat and add eggs. Mix & add cream cheese once eggs are nearly cooked. Set aside.
6. Add bacon/eggs mixture to pizza crust. Top with shredded cheese and air fry for 5 mins until cheese melted and bubbly.

220kcal, Fat: 13g, Carbohydrates: 17g, Protein:13g

BREAKFAST MAC & CHEESE

Serving Size	Prep Time	Cooking time	Total Time
4 Servings	15 Minutes	10 Minutes	25 Minutes

Ingredients

- 225g elbow macaroni
- 225g shredded cheddar cheese
- 500ml whole milk
- 125ml heavy cream
- 3 tbsp butter
- ¾ tsp mustard powder
- ⅛ tsp nutmeg
- Salt & pepper to taste

Directions

1. Preheat the Air fryer to 350°F/176°C. Spray a 20cm cake pan (10cm deep) with cooking spray.
2. Add all the ingredients (except butter) to the pan. Mix until all combined.
3. Put in the air fryer.
4. Air fry for 20 minutes (Stirring every 8 minutes). After 15 minutes add butter and stir.
5. Remove from the air fryer and let rest for 5 minutes. Serve.

Calories: 380kcal, Carbohydrates: 47g, Protein: 26g, Fat: 27g, Fiber: 2g, Sugar: 8g.

BRUSSELS SPROUTS APPLE NUT SALAD

Serving Size	Prep Time	Cooking time	Total Time
5 Servings	15 Minutes	15 Minutes	30 Minutes

Ingredients

- 450g Brussels sprouts trimmed and halved
- 2 tbsp olive oil
- Salt & Pepper to Taste½ tsp cayenne pepper
- 125g chopped apple
- 30g chopped nuts
- 80ml red wine vinaigrette

Directions

1. Preheat air fryer to 350°F/175°C for 5 minutes.
2. In a bowl, add brussels sprouts olive oil, salt, pepper, and cayenne pepper. Mix.
3. Place brussels sprouts in air fryer basket and cook for 15 minutes. Stir halfway through cooking time and add in apple, and chopped nuts. Cook for more 4 minutes.
4. Remove from air fryer and transfer to a serving plate. Drizzle with red wine vinaigrette. Serve.

Calories: 222kcal | Carbohydrates: 27g | Protein: 4g | Fat: 13g | Sodium: 140mg | Fiber: 5g | Sugar: 17g

SCOTCH EGG

Serving Size	Prep Time	Cooking time	Total Time
4 Servings	25 Minutes	10 Minutes	35 Minutes

Ingredients

- 500g minced beef, (90% lean)
- 5 eggs
- 1 tsp. dried sage
- 1/2 tsp red chili flake
- 1/2 tsp garlic powder
- 1/2 tsp onion powder
- 60g plain flour
- 2 tbsp milk
- 60g panko bread crumbs
- Cooking spray
- Salt & pepper to taste

Directions

1. In medium saucepan over high heat.bring 1 liter of water to a boil; add 4 eggs, boil 5 minutes. Then transfer boiled eggs into a large bowl full with ice water.
2. In a large mixing bowl, add minced beef, all the spices and season with salt & pepper. Mix until all combined.
3. Peel the eggs. Divide the minced beef into 4 portions and form into 1/2cm thick disks. Place the egg in the middle of each disk. Wrap the beef around each egg to fully cover the egg with beef.
4. Prepare three bowls: 1) with flour, 2) egg whisked with milk, and 3) panko. Dredge each egg in flour, dip in egg then roll in panko. Refrigerate Scotch egg for 20 minutes.
5. Set air fryer to 390°F/200°C. Spray each Scotch egg with cooking spray and place in air fryer. Air fry for 8 minutes, flip and air fry for more 7 minutes.

400kcal, Fat: 13g, Carbohydrates: 20g, Protein:44g

SALAMI & CHEESE QUESADILLA

Serving Size	Prep Time	Cooking time	Total Time
1 Servings	4 Minutes	6 Minutes	10 Minutes

Ingredients

- 2 tortillas
- 6 slices Salami or protein of your choice
- 30g cheese any flavor of cheese - Monterey jack cheese, or Mozzarella cheese
- olive oil

Directions

1. Spray air fryer basket with cooking spray.
2. Place tortilla in the air fryer basket. Add ham, cheese, then another tortilla. Spray with cooking spray.
3. Keep the quesadilla down with tooth picks.
4. Air fry at 360°F/182°C for 6 minutes until tortilla is crispy.

Calories: 435kcal | Carbohydrates: 30g | Protein: 24g | Fat: 24g | Sodium: 1291mg | Fiber: 2g |

AVOCADO TOAST

Serving Size	Prep Time	Cooking time	Total Time
2 Servings	7 Minutes	3 Minutes	10 Minutes

Ingredients

- 1 slice bread frozen, bread of your choice
- 1 avocado
- lime juice to taste
- 1 tomato
- sausage

Directions

1. Cook the sausage strips in the air fryer at 400°F/205°C for 6 minutes.
2. Place frozen piece of bread in air fryer basket. spray it with cooking spray. Toast at 380°F/193°C for 3 minutes.
3. In a bowl, mash up avocado with a fork. Add lime juice to taste.
4. Slice the tomato.
5. Layer the toasted piece of toast with avocado, tomato slices, then sausage.

Calories: 419kcal | Carbohydrates: 24g | Protein: 14g | Fat: 31g | Sodium: 499mg | Fiber: 9g | Sugar: 4g

BAKED POTATO

Serving Size	Prep Time	Cooking time	Total Time
2 Servings	1 Minutes	45 Minutes	50 Minutes

Ingredients

- 2 (227g each) Russet potatoes
- 2 tsp oil
- Salt & pepper to taste

Optional Toppings
- sour cream
- butter
- green onions or chives
- cheese

Directions

1. Poke holes with a fork on both sides of the potato. Brush the potato skin with oil. Roll each potato on salt.
2. Place the potatoes in air fryer basket and cook at 445°F/230°C for 45 mins.
3. When time up, remove the potatoes from the basket, cut a slit or two in the top.
4. Top with all your favorite toppings and enjoy!

Per Serving: 219kcal
Fat: 5g, Carbohydrates: 40g, Protein:8g

HEALTHY BAKED SALMON

Serving Size	Prep Time	Cooking time	Total Time
2 Servings	10 Minutes	10 Minutes	20 Minutes

Ingredients

- Two (170g each) salmon fillets, (skin & bones removed, rinsed & patted dry)
- 1 tsp. olive oil
- Salt & pepper to taste
- Cooking spray

Directions

1. Coat salmon fillets with oil , then Season both sides with salt & pepper.
2. Spray air fryer basket with cooking spray.
3. Put salmon fillets in air fryer basket. Air fry at 370°F/187°C for 10 minutes.
4. Serve.

calories: 259kcal, protein: 33g, fat: 12g

AIR FRYER SALMON

Serving Size	Prep Time	Cooking time	Total Time
4 Servings	8 Minutes	12 Minutes	20 Minutes

Ingredients

- 4 salmon fillets

Marinade

- 3 Tbsp maple syrup
- 4 tsp soy sauce
- 2 garlic cloves, (minced
- Salt & pepper to taste

Directions

1. In a bowl, add maple syrup, soy sauce, garlic, season with salt & pepper. Mix until combined.
2. Add salmon fillets to marinade mixture. refrigerate for 30 minutes.
3. Spray air fryer basket with cooking spray. Add salmon fillets and spread into single layer.
4. Air Fry at 347°F/175°C for 12 minutes.
5. Serve warm.

Per Serving: calories: 200kcal, carbohydrates: 10g, protein: 25g, fat: 7g, sugar: 8g.

AIR FRIED SHRIMP

Serving Size	Prep Time	Cooking time	Total Time
6 Servings	10 Minutes	10 Minutes	20 Minutes

Ingredients

- 24 Jumbo shrimp, (shell removed)
- 2 large eggs
- 30g plain flour
- 100g breadcrumbs
- 2 tsp oil
- 1 tsp onion powder
- 1 tsp garlic powder
- 2 tsp paprika
- Salt & pepper to taste
- Cooking spray

Directions

1. Preheat your air fryer to 347°F/220°C.
2. In a medium bowl, add flour. In Another bowl, add eggs, whisk until combined. In a third bowl, mix all of seasonings and breadcrumbs.
3. Coat each shrimp in flour. Then dip in egg. Finally dredge in breadcrumbs. Repeat for all shrimp.
4. Spray air fryer basket with cooking spray. Put shrimp in a single layer, in air fryer basket, Spray top of the shrimp with cooking spray.
5. Air fry at 370°F/190°C for 8 minutes until golden brown.
6. When time is up, remove from air fryer, and serve.

Calories: 211kcal, Carbohydrates: 19g, Protein: 21g, Fat: 5g, Fiber: 1g, Sugar: 1g

PRAWN FAJITAS

Serving Size	Prep Time	Cooking time	Total Time
4 Servings	8 Minutes	22 Minutes	30 Minutes

Ingredients

- 900g medium prawn, (tail-off & defrosted)
- 1 red bell pepper, (chopped)
- 1 green bell pepper, (chopped)
- 1 onion, (chopped)
- 2 tbsp. fajita or taco seasoning
- Cooking spray
- Salt & pepper to taste
- Corn/flour tortillas

Directions

1. Spray the air fryer basket with cooking spray.
2. Add the peppers, onion, and seasoning to the basket. Mix it together. Then spray evenly with cooking spray. Cook at 400°F/205°C for 11 minutes.
3. Add the prawn. Spray it with cooking spray and mix together. Cook for another 10 minutes.
4. Serve on its own or with tortillas.

88kcal, Fat: 2g, Carbohydrates: 6g, Protein:10g

FISH & CHIPS

Serving Size	Prep Time	Cooking time	Total Time
6 Servings	10 Minutes	8 Minutes	18 Minutes

Ingredients

- 900g cod fillets
- 60g flour
- 30g cornstarch
- 1 tbsp sugar
- 120ml cold water
- 1 egg
- 100g plain flour
- 100g breadcrumbs
- Salt & pepper to taste
- Cooking spray

For the chips
- 1¼ kg, peeled and cut into 1/2 inch/1.5cm long fries
- Salt & pepper to taste

Directions

1. Soak potatoes in a bowl of cold water for 30 minutes.
2. In a bowl, whisk 60g flour and cornstarch. In another bowl, stir together 100g flour, garlic powder, onion powder, salt, pepper, and baking soda. Pour in cold water and stir to combine. (if too thick add more water)
3. Dredge each fish piece in flour mixture, then in the batter. Place the fish pieces back in the flour mixture to fully coat.
4. Line air fryer basket with parchment paper and spray with cooking spray.add fish into basket. (work in batches) Spray tops of fish with cooking spray. Cook at 400°F/200°C for 5 minutes. Flip and spray with cooking spray. Air fry for 4 minutes,until golden brown.
5. Remove from air fryer to a plate and cover with foil. Set aside.
6. drain potatoes and dry them with a towel. spray air fryer basket with cooking spray. Place and spray with cooking spray. Air fry the potatoes at 400°F/200°C for 7 minutes. Flip, cook for 7 minutes unti golden brown and crispy. Sprinkle with salt and pepper. Serve the fish and chips.

Calories: 211kcal, Carbohydrates: 19g, Protein: 21g, Fat: 5g, Fiber: 1g, Sugar: 1g

WHITE FISH WITH GARLIC & LEMON

Serving Size	Prep Time	Cooking time	Total Time
5 Servings	7 Minutes	8 Minutes	15 Minutes

Ingredients

- 340g white fish fillets
- 1/2 tsp garlic powder
- 3 tsp lemon juice
- 1/2 tsp onion powder
- 1 tsp smoked paprika
- Salt & pepper to taste
- fresh chopped parsley
- Cooking spray

Directions

1. Preheat air fryer to 360°F/180°C for 5 minutes.
2. Spray fish fillets with cooking spray and season with garlic powder, lemon juice, onion power, paprika salt and pepper. Repeat for both sides.
3. Spray air fryer basket with cooking spray. Put the fish on the basket.
4. Air fry for 8 minutes. Cooking time depend on the thickness of the fillets.
5. Remove from air fryer. Sprinkle with chopped parsley and serve.

calories: 169kcal, carbohydrates: 1g, protein: 34g, fat: 3g, fiber: 1g, sugar: 1g.

SWAI FISH

Serving Size	Prep Time	Cooking time	Total Time
2 Servings	10 Minutes	7 Minutes	17 Minutes

Ingredients

- 2 (115g each) Swai filets
- 1 tsp olive oil
- 1 ½ tbsp. paprika
- ½ tbsp. garlic powder
- ½ tbsp. onion powder
- ½ tbsp. dried thyme
- ½ tsp. cayenne pepper
- ½ tsp. dried basil
- ½ tsp. dried oregano
- Salt & pepper to taste
- Cooking spray

Directions

1. Preheat the air fryer to 400°F/200°C. Spray the air fryer basket with cooking spray.
2. Spray both sides of the fish fillets with cooking spray. Sprinkle blackened seasoning onto both sides of the fish.
3. Put fish fillets into the air fryer basket and air fry for 7 minutes, flip and air fry for another 4 minutes
4. Serve with your favorite side.

Calories: 100kcal, Protein: 21g, Fat: 1g

SHRIMP COCKTAIL

Serving Size	Prep Time	Cooking time	Total Time
6 Servings	5 Minutes	12 Minutes	17 Minutes

Ingredients

FOR THE SHRIMP

- 500g shrimp, (deveined & shells removed)
- 1 tsp oil

SHRIMP COCKTAIL SAUCE

- 120g ketchup
- 2 tsp Worcestershire sauce
- 1 tsp fresh lemon juice
- 1/4 tsp celery salt
- 1/4 tsp garlic powder
- Salt & pepper to taste

Directions

1. In a small mixing bowl, add ketchup, Worcestershire sauce, lemon juice, celery salt, garlic powder, season with salt & pepper. Mix until combined. Set aside.
2. Coat shrimp with oil, and season with salt & pepper.
3. Put the shrimp in the air fryer basket in a single layer.
4. Air fry shrimp at 400°F/200°C for 12 minutes.
5. Remove from air fryer, let shrimp cool completely.
6. Serve with the shrimp cocktail sauce.

calories: 89kcal, carbohydrates: 2g, protein: 16g, fat: 2g, fiber: 1g, sugar: 1g.

SALMON FAJITAS

Serving Size	Prep Time	Cooking time	Total Time
4 Servings	5 Minutes	10 Minutes	15 Minutes

Ingredients

- 2-4 salmon fillets
- Cooking spray
- 1 fajita seasoning
- 340 g bag frozen peppers and onions
- Flour tortillas

Toppings
- 1-2 avocados
- 1-2 limes
- 1 package coleslaw mix
- salsa or pico de gallo

Directions

1. Pat the salmon dry with paper towels.
2. Place the salmon on a foil sling and surround it with the peppers and onions in the air fryer basket. Lightly spray with cooking spray and massage salmon with fajita seasoning.
3. Cook at 350°F/175°C for 10 minutes until salmon flakes easily and registers at 145°F/62.8°C.
4. Remove from air fryer and serve on tortillas with avocado, salsa, lime, coleslaw, etc.

Calories: 289kcal | Carbohydrates: 24g | Protein: 22g | Fat: 13g | Sodium: 122mg | Fiber: 10g | Sugar: 4g

PARMESAN CRUSTED SALMON

Serving Size	Prep Time	Cooking time	Total Time
8 Servings	5 Minutes	8 Minutes	13 Minutes

Ingredients

- 2 salmon fillets
- 60g mayonnaise
- 1 tsp garlic powder
- 1 tsp onion powder
- 1 tsp dried basil
- 1 tsp dried oregano
- 1 tsp dried thyme
- shredded parmesan cheese to taste

Directions

1. Preheat the air fryer at 400°F/204°C.
2. in a small bowl, mix mayonnaise, and seasoning.
3. Pat dry the salmon fillets with a paper towel and place the salmon in a sprayed air fryer basket.
4. Spread the herb mayonnaise mixture on the top of the salmon filets. Top with parmesan cheese.
5. Cook at 350°F/175°C for 8 minutes until the salmon registers at 145°F/62.7°C with an instant read thermometer.

Calories: 219kcal | Carbohydrates: 1g | Protein: 17g | Fat: 16g | Sodium: 127mg | Fiber: 1g | Sugar: 1g

CRISPY FISH FILLETS

Serving Size	Prep Time	Cooking time	Total Time
4 Servings	5 Minutes	15 Minutes	20 Minutes

Ingredients

- 450g white fish fillets (not more than ½ inch/1.5cm thick)
- 1 large egg
- 60g yellow cornmeal
- 1 tsp paprika
- ½ tsp garlic powder
- ½ tsp black pepper
- 1 tsp salt
- cooking spray
- lemon for garnish

Directions

1. Preheat air fryer to 400 F.
2. in a shallow bowl, Whisk egg . In another bowl, combine cornmeal and spices.
3. Pat fish completely dry. Dip fish fillets into the egg. Then press fish into cornmeal mixture until coated on both sides.
4. Place fish into air fryer basket. Spray with cooking spray. Cook for 10 minutes, flip halfway through cooking time. If its not fully cooked, return to air fryer and cook 7 minutes.
5. Once done, squeeze with lemon. Serve immediately.

calories: 191kcal, carbohydrates: 15g, protein: 24g, fat: 3g, fiber: 2g, sugar: 1g.

MAHI MAHI

Serving Size	Prep Time	Cooking time	Total Time
2 Servings	5 Minutes	10 Minutes	15 Minutes

Ingredients

- 2 (170g each) mahi mahi fish fillets skin removed
- 1 tbsp olive oil
- ½ tsp paprika
- ½ tsp salt
- ½ tsp garlic powder
- ¼ tsp ground black pepper

Directions

1. Pat the mahi mahi dry on both sides. Cover mahi mahi with oil.
2. In a small bowl, mix paprika, salt, garlic powder and ground black pepper .
3. Then, gently rub the spices onto the mahi mahi filets.
4. Place mahi mahi filets in air fryer basket. Air fry at 400°F/205°C for 10 minutes until the mahi mahi reaches an internal temperature of 137°F.

calories: 67kcal, carbohydrates: 1g, protein: 1g, fat: 7g, fiber: 1g, sugar: 1g | Sodium: 583mg.

CATFISH

Serving Size	Prep Time	Cooking time	Total Time
4 Servings	10 Minutes	20 Minutes	50 Minutes

Ingredients

- 900g catfish filets
- 240 g buttermilk
- 5 to 6 drops hot sauce
- 160g yellow cornmeal
- 42g all-purpose flour
- 2 tbsp Cajun seasoning
- 1/2 tsp black pepper

Directions

1. Whisk buttermilk and hot sauce. Cover catfish filets completely with marinate in ziplock bag in the refrigerator for 20 minutes.
2. In a bowl, whisk cornmeal, flour, Cajun seasoning, and pepper.
3. After marinating, let fish drain in colander.
4. Dredge the fillets through the cornmeal mixture, coating each side evenly. Let rest on a baking sheet for 10 minutes.
5. Put a single layer of fillets in the air fryer basket and spray the tops with cooking spray. Cook in batches.
6. Air fry at 375°F/1905°C for 10 minutes, then flip, spray again, and cook another 10 minutes. Serve with greens.

calories: 454kcal, carbohydrates: 42g, protein: 45g, fat: 11g, fiber: 1g, sugar: 4g | Sodium: 198mg.

TILAPIA

Serving Size	Prep Time	Cooking time	Total Time
4 Servings	10 Minutes	12 Minutes	22 Minutes

Ingredients

- 4 tilapia filets
- Spray oil
- 1 tsp chili powder
- 0.5 tsp garlic salt
- 0.5 tsp pepper
- 110 g breadcrumbs

Directions

1. Spray tilaipa fillets with a little bit of oil and set aside.
2. Combine spices in small bowl.
3. Put breadcrumbs in ziplock bag. Add spices to bag and shake well to combine.
4. One at a time, place tilapia into bag and gently press breadcrumb mixture into the fish. repeat for each filet.
5. Cook fillets at 400°F/205°C for 12 minutes in air fryer basket. Flip fillets halfway through cooking.

calories: 109kcal, carbohydrates: 20g, protein: 4g, fat: 2g, fiber: 1g, sugar: 2g | Sodium: 63mg.

SHRIMP AND VEGETABLES

Serving Size	Prep Time	Cooking time	Total Time
4 Servings	25 Minutes	20 Minutes	25 Minutes

Ingredients

- Small Shrimp Peeled & Deveined
- 1 Bag of Frozen Mixed Vegetables
- 1 Tbsp Cajun Seasoning
- Cooking Spray
- Cooked Rice

Directions

1. Add the shrimp and vegetables to air fryer.
2. Top it with Cajun seasoning and spray with cooking spray.
3. Cook on 355°F/180°C for 10 minutes.
4. open and mix shrimp and vegetables.
5. Continue cooking for an additional 10 minutes.
6. Serve over rice.

calories: 100kcal, carbohydrates: 15g, protein: 2g, fat: 4g, fiber: 1g, sugar: 4g | Sodium: 837mg.

TUNA MELT

Serving Size	Prep Time	Cooking time	Total Time
4 Servings	10 Minutes	6 Minutes	16 Minutes

Ingredients

- 360g can of tuna fish
- 2 tbsp mayonnaise
- dill pickle relish
- 4-8 slices bread
- 1-2 tomatoes sliced
- ½ stick butter
- 2-4 cheese slices, Cheddar cheese, Provolone cheese, or Swiss cheese

Directions

1. Combine the tuna with mayonnaise. add pickle relish to tuna mixture.
2. Butter each slice of bread. Place slices of bread, butter side down, in air fryer basket.
3. Layer each slice of bread with tuna, tomato slices, cheese slices, and then top with slice of bread with butter side on outside.
4. Cook at 350°F/175°C for 6 minutes until bread is browned and cheese is melted. flip at the halfway point.
5. remove from the air fryer basket and serve.

Calories: 347kcal | Carbohydrates: 16g | Protein: 22g | Fat: 21g | Sodium: 526mg | Fiber: 2g | Sugar: 3g

FISH TACOS

Serving Size	Prep Time	Cooking time	Total Time
4 Servings	20 Minutes	12 Minutes	32 Minutes

Ingredients

- 720g firm white fish fillets
- 1 tbsp grill seasoning
- 40g onion finely chopped
- 2 tbsp fresh cilantro finely chopped
- 1 tsp salt divided
- 60g mayonnaise
- 60g chipotle sauce
- 1 tbsp fresh lime juice
- corn tortillas

Directions

1. Stir onion, cilantro and half tsp salt. Set aside.
2. Stir the mayonnaise, chipotle sauce, lime juice and remaining half tsp of salt. Set aside.
3. Evenly sprinkle the fish with the grill seasoning.
4. Brush the air fryer basket lightly with vegetable oil to prevent sticking.
5. Arrange the fish in a single layer in the basket. Cook at 400°F/200°C for 12 minutes until the internal temperature of the fish reaches 145°F.
6. Serve the fish with corn tortillas, the salsa and chipotle mayonnaise.

SALMON BITES

Serving Size	Prep Time	Cooking time	Total Time
2 Servings	5 Minutes	8 Minutes	15 Minutes

Ingredients

Lemon Dill Sauce

- 145g plain Greek yogurt
- 2 tbsp lemon juice
- ½ tbsp olive oil
- 2 tbsp fresh chopped dill
- ½ tbsp dijon mustard
- ¼ tsp garlic powder
- salt & pepper to taste

Salmon Bites

- 720g salmon fillets
- 1 tsp avocado oil
- ½ tsp garlic powder
- salt and pepper to taste

Directions

1. Pat salmon fillets dry. remove the skin. cut the fillets into cubes.
2. Place salmon into a bowl. Add avocado oil, garlic powder, salt and pepper. combine until pieces evenly coated.
3. Place salmon into air fryer basket. Do not put them on top of one another.
4. Air fry at 370°F/190°C for 10 minutes.
5. Combine all the ingredients for the sauce in a bowl.
6. Serve the bites with pasta or salad or on its own with sauce.

CAJUN SHRIMP

Serving Size	Prep Time	Cooking time	Total Time
4 Servings	20 Minutes	12 Minutes	32 Minutes

Ingredients

- 1 tbsp Cajun seasoning
- 450g cleaned and peeled extra jumbo shrimp
- 180g cooked Turkey/Chicken sausage, sliced
- 1 medium zucchini, sliced into 1/4-inch/0.5cm thick half moons
- 1 medium yellow squash, 180g sliced into 1/4-inch/0.5cm thick half moons
- 1 large red bell pepper, seeded and cut into thin 1-inch/2.5cm pieces
- 1/4 tsp salt
- 2 tbsp olive oil

Directions

1. In a large bowl, add Cajun seasoning and shrimp, toss to coat.
2. Add sausage, zucchini, squash, bell peppers, and salt and toss with the oil.
3. Preheat the air fryer 400°F/205°C
4. In 2 batches, transfer the shrimp and vegetables to air fryer basket and cook 8 minutes, shaking the basket 3 times during cooking process.
5. Set aside, repeat with remaining shrimp and veggies.

calories: 284kcal, carbohydrates: 8g, protein: 31g, fat: 11g, fiber: 2g, sugar: 3g | Sodium: 1500mg.

SALMON BURGERS

Serving Size	Prep Time	Cooking time	Total Time
4 Servings	20 Minutes	13 Minutes	1 hour 33 minutes

Ingredients

- 450g fresh salmon
- 2 tbsp Dijon mustard
- 1 tbsp mayonnaise
- 1 tbsp lemon juice
- 40g panko breadcrumbs
- 2 tbsp scallions chopped (or yellow onion or shallot)
- ¼ tsp crushed red chili flakes
- salt and pepper to taste
- cooking spray

Directions

1. Remove any skin and bones from salmon, then chop into pieces. Transfer 1/4 of salmon pieces to a food processor. Place remaining salmon in a large bowl.
2. Add mustard, mayonnaise, and lemon juice to the food processor. Pulse until a thick paste forms. Transfer mixture to bowl with remaining salmon. Mix in bread crumbs, scallions, and chili flakes until evenly combined.
3. Form salmon mixture into 4 patties. Place on a baking sheet and season with salt and pepper. Place in the freezer for 1 hour.
4. Preheat air fryer to 400°F/200°C. Spray air fryer basket with cooking spray
5. Place burgers in basket and spray tops with cooking spray. Cook for 8 minutes. flip, spray tops again and cook for 5 minutes.

Calories: 236kcal | Carbohydrates: 9g | Protein: 24g | Fat: 11g | Sodium: 240mg | Fiber: 1g | Sugar: 1g

HONEY GLAZED SALMON

Serving Size	Prep Time	Cooking time	Total Time
4 Servings	2 Minutes	8 Minutes	10 Minutes

Ingredients

- 4 Salmon Fillets, skin on
- Salt & Pepper to taste
- 2 tsp Soy Sauce
- 1 tbsp Honey
- 1 tsp Sesame Seeds

Directions

1. Preheat the air fryer 375°F/190°C.
2. Season each salmon fillet with salt and pepper. Brush the soy sauce into the fish.
3. Place the fillets into air fryer basket skin side down and cook for 8 minutes.
4. About a minute or two before the time is up, glaze each fillet with honey and sprinkle with sesame seeds. Put them back in and finish cooking.
5. Serve with a side of your choice.

calories: 262kcal, carbohydrates: 5g, protein: 2g, fat: 11g, fiber: 1g, sugar: 4g | Sodium: 158mg.

HONEY LIME SHRIMP

Serving Size	Prep Time	Cooking time	Total Time
2 Servings	5 Minutes	5 Minutes	40 Minutes

Ingredients

- 450g large shrimp raw; remove shell and tail
- 1 ½ tbsp olive oil
- 1 ½ tbsp lime juice
- 1 ½ tbsp honey
- 2 cloves garlic minced
- ⅛ tsp salt

To Garnish
- lime wedges
- cilantro

Directions

1. In a large bowl, stir oil, lime juice, honey, garlic and salt. Add shrimp and marinate for 30 minutes.
2. Heat the air fryer 390°F/200°C. Shake excess marinade off shrimp and put in the air fryer.
3. Cook for 2 minutes, shake. Cook for another 3 minutes.
4. Serve - with lime wedges and cilantro.

calories: 187kcal, carbohydrates: 7g, protein: 23g, fat: 7g, sugar: 7g | Sodium: 955mg.

COCONUT SHRIMP WITH ORANGE DIPPING

Serving Size	Prep Time	Cooking time	Total Time
3 Servings	10 Minutes	15 Minutes	25 Minutes

Ingredients

- 500g large shrimp, (peeled & deveined)
- 1/2 tsp smoked paprika
- 1/2 tsp garlic powder
- 50g flour
- 2 eggs
- 50g coconut flakes
- 60g breadcrumbs

For the sauce

- 80g orange marmalade
- 1 tbsp chili garlic sauce
- 1 tbsp rice vinegar
- 1 tsp soy sauce

Directions

1. In a large mixing bowl, add shrimp, paprika, garlic powder, salt & pepper. Mix until all sides of shrimp coated with seasoning.
2. In a large mixing bowl, add flour. In another bowl, add eggs, whisk them. In third bowl add coconut flakes and breadcrumbs.
3. Dip each shrimp into the flour, then eggs and then into the breadcrumbs.
4. Spray air fryer basket with cooking spray. Put the shrimp in a single layer in the air fryer basket. Spray the top of shrimp with cooking spray.
5. Air Fry at 370°F/190°C for 14 minutes, flipping halfway through cooking time.
6. Whisk together the all of the dipping sauce ingredients until smooth. Serve with the shrimp.

calories: 199kcal, carbohydrates: 22g, protein: 19g, fat: 4g, fiber: 1g, sugar: 11g

FRIED SHRIMP

Serving Size	Prep Time	Cooking time	Total Time
4 Servings	15 Minutes	12 Minutes	27 Minutes

Ingredients

- 450g uncooked large shrimp, thawed if frozen, peeled & deveined
- 60g all-purpose flour
- 1 tsp seasoning salt
- 2 large eggs
- 100g panko breadcrumbs
- Cooking spray

Directions

1. Combine flour and seasoning salt in a shallow dish or bowl. beat eggs in a second bowl. Place panko bread crumbs in a third bowl.
2. Preheat air fryer to 400°F/204°C.
3. coat shrimp first in flour mixture, then dip in egg, then coat shrimp completely in panko. Place on a plate.
4. Spray with cooking spray. Arrange the shrimp in the air fryer with plenty of space around each one. Air fry for 6 minutes until golden brown . Transfer to a serving plate and repeat with the remaining shrimp.

BANG BANG SHRIMP

Serving Size	Prep Time	Cooking time	Total Time
4 Servings	10 Minutes	8 Minutes	18 Minutes

Ingredients

- 12 frozen peeled and deveined shrimp thawed
- 1 large egg
- 60g mayonnaise divided
- 2 tbsp lime juice divided
- 80g Panko bread crumbs
- 3 tbsp sweet chili sauce
- 1 tbsp Siraracha
- pinch of salt

Directions

1. pat dry shrimp with paper towels. Sprinkle shrimp salt.
2. In a shallow bowl, whisk together egg, 2 tbsp mayonnaise and one tbsp lime juice. In another bowl, add Panko bread crumbs.
3. Dip each shrimp into egg mixture and then int bread crumbs.
4. Place breaded shrimp into air fryer basket, making sure they are not touching.
5. Air fry at 400°F/204°C for 8 minutes.
6. While the shrimp is cooking, whisk remaining mayonnaise and lime juice with sweet chili sauce, Siraracha sauce and a pinch of salt. Serve the sauce with shrimp.

CRAB CAKES

Serving Size	Prep Time	Cooking time	Total Time
4 Servings	10 Minutes	10 Minutes	20 Minutes

Ingredients

- 450g lump crabmeat
- 60g mayonnaise
- 30g Panko
- 60g flour
- 1 large egg
- 2 tbsp green onion sliced
- 1/2 red bell pepper finely diced
- 1 tbsp Worcestershire sauce
- 1 tbsp cajun
- juice of half lemon

Directions

1. In a large bowl add crabmeat, mayonnaise, Panko, flour, egg, green onion, bell pepper, Worcestershire sauce, cajun, and lemon juice . Mix and shape into patties.
2. Place in air fryer basket. Cook at 360°F/182°C for 12 minutes until golden brown

calories: 275kcal, carbohydrates: 13g, protein: 25g, fat: 4g, fiber: 13g, sugar: 1g

SALMON AND POTATOES BAKE

Serving Size	Prep Time	Cooking time	Total Time
4 Servings	5 Minutes	10 Minutes	15 Minutes

Ingredients

- 225g red potatoes, cut into bite size pieces
- 225g brussels sprouts, halved
- 4 tbsp oil divided
- 5 tbsp your favorite seasoning mix divided
- 800g salmon fillets

Directions

1. Combine the potatoes in a large bowl with 2½ tbsp oil and 3½ tbsp Seasoning Mix until coated.
2. Place potatoes in air fryer basket and cook at 350°F/176°C for 7 minutes.
3. brush salmon fillets both sides with remaining oil, and season with remaining Seasoning.
4. Stir potatoes . Add salmon on top and cook at 350°F/176°C for 10 minutes.
5. Remove salmon from the air fryer basket. Serve..

Calories: 238kcal | Carbohydrates: 27g | Protein: 5g | Fat: 15g | Sodium: 29mg | Fiber: 11g | Sugar: 3g

SHRIMP TACOS

Serving Size	Prep Time	Cooking time	Total Time
4 Servings	3 Minutes	7 Minutes	10 Minutes

Ingredients

- 450g small shrimp raw, peeled, deveined, tails-off
- 1 tbsp oil
- ¾ tsp chili powder
- ¾ tsp garlic powder
- ½ tsp cumin
- ½ tsp onion powder
- pinch of salt and pepper

Toppings

- 4 flour tortillas or corn tortillas
- green shredded cabbage
- sliced avocados
- crumbled feta cheese
- lime

Directions

1. in a bowl.Toss shrimp with oil, chili powder, garlic powder, cumin, onion powder, salt & pepper.
2. Place shrimp in air fryer basket. Cook at 400°F/204°C for 8 minutes or until shrimp is cooked through.
3. assemble tortillas with shrimp, cabbage, and cheese . Place in air fryer basket and cook at 400°F/204°C for 1 minute.
4. Remove tacos from the air fryer, add the toppings and serve.

Calories: 208kcal | Carbohydrates: 17g | Protein: 18g | Fat: 7g | Sodium: 879mg | Fiber: 1g | Sugar: 1g

SHEPHERD'S PIE

Serving Size	Prep Time	Cooking time	Total Time
6 Servings	20 Minutes	10 Minutes	30 Minutes

Ingredients

- 340g boneless, skinless chicken breasts
- ¼ tsp salt
- ¼ tsp black pepper
- 340g jar chicken gravy
- 280g frozen mixed vegetables thawed
- ½ tsp onion powder
- 420 g prepared mashed potatoes
- 2 tbsp butter melted

Directions

1. Coat air fryer basket with cooking spray. Sprinkle chicken with salt and pepper, place in basket, and air fry 5 minutes at 380°F/190°C. Turn chicken over and cook 6 minutes until no pink remains in center. Remove to cutting board, let cool slightly, and cut into 1/2-inch/ 1.5cm chunks.
2. in a skillet over medium heat, combine gravy, vegetables, onion powder, salt, and pepper. Cook 7 minutes. When chicken is ready, add chicken to gravy mixture and spoon mixture evenly into 4 ramekins.
3. Top each ramekin with mashed potatoes and drizzle melted butter on top. air fry until the top is golden.

Calories: 356kcal | Carbohydrates: 38g | Protein: 23g | Fat: 13g | Sodium: 733mg | Fiber: 5g | Sugar: 2g

ROSEMARY RANCH CHICKEN

Serving Size	Prep Time	Cooking time	Total Time
4 Servings	10 Minutes	15 Minutes	8 hours 25 minutes

Ingredients

- 1 tbsp olive oil
- 120g ranch salad dressing
- 65g Worcestershire sauce
- 2 tbsp fresh lemon juice
- 1 tbsp finely chopped fresh rosemary
- 1 tsp salt
- ¼ tsp black pepper
- 680g chicken breasts about 2-4 chicken breasts

Directions

1. whisk together all the ingredients except the chicken until combined.
2. To even out chicken, pound the thicker side down so chicken will cook evenly.
3. Place chicken in shallow dish and pour the marinade over the chicken. Cover and refrigerate for 8-12 hours.
4. Place chicken in air fryer basket in a single layer.
5. Air fry at 380°F/190°C for 13 minutes, turning at the halfway point.
6. let the chicken rest for 5-10 minutes to finish cooking, then slice and serve.

Calories: 451kcal | Carbohydrates: 6g | Protein: 49g | Fat: 25g | Sodium: 1341mg | Fiber: 1g | Sugar: 3g

CHEESY CHICKEN SAUSAGE ROLLS

Serving Size	Prep Time	Cooking time	Total Time
24 Servings	30 Minutes	15 Minutes	45 Minutes

Ingredients

- 500g chicken mince
- 125g can corn kernels, (drained & roughly chopped)
- 1 medium grated zucchini
- 1 small grated carrot
- 50g grated cheddar cheese
- 30g breadcrumbs
- 1 green onion, (chopped)
- 1 garlic clove, (minced)
- 3 sheets frozen puff pastry, (thawed & halved)
- 1 egg, (beaten)
- Salt & pepper to taste
- Sesame seeds, to sprinkle
- Cooking spray

Directions

1. In a large mixing bowl, add chicken mince, corn kernels, zucchini, carrot, cheddar cheese, breadcrumbs, green onion, garlic, and season with salt & pepper. Mix until combine.
2. Put 1 pastry half on a flat surface. Spoon 1/3 cup mince mixture, put on pastry. Brush edges with egg. Roll up to form a log. Trim ends. Cut into 4 equal pieces. Repeat.
3. Brush rolls with egg and sprinkle with sesame seeds.
4. Spray air fryer with cooking spray, Put rolls in the basket.
5. Cook at 400°F/200°C, in batches, for 15 minutes until golden.
6. Serve with sweet chilli sauce.

Calories: 90kcal, Carbohydrates: 5.5g, Protein: 8g, Fat: 4g, Fiber: 0.5g, Sugar: 0.7g

BAKED CHICKEN BREAST

Serving Size	Prep Time	Cooking time	Total Time
3 Servings	6 Minutes	20 Minutes	26 Minutes

Ingredients

- 3 boneless chicken breasts, (200g each)
- 2 tbsp lemon juice
- 1 tbsp olive oil
- ½ tsp chili powder
- ½ tsp cumin
- ¼ tsp garlic powder
- Salt & pepper to taste

Directions

1. Preheat the Air fryer to 380°F/193°C.
2. In a large mixing bowl, add chicken, oil, lemon juice, chili powder, cumin, garlic powder and season with salt & pepper. Mix until all chicken coated.
3. Put in the air fryer in a single layer.
4. Air fry for 20 minutes. Flipping halfway through cooking time.
5. Remove from the air fryer and let rest for 5 minutes. Serve.

240kcal, Carbohydrates: 1g, Protein: 24g, Fat: 15g, Fiber: 1g, Sugar: 1g.

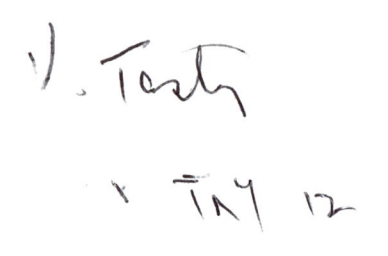

DUCK

Serving Size	Prep Time	Cooking time	Total Time
4 Servings	10 Minutes	60 Minutes	75 Minutes

Ingredients

- 1 (1300g) whole duck, (thawed)
- 2 tbsp. olive oil
- 1 tbsp. rosemary, (chopped)
- 1 tsp. thyme
- 2 garlic cloves, (minced)
- Salt & pepper to taste

Directions

1. Remove the duck neck and any giblets. Rinse, and pat dry with paper towels. Set aside.
2. In a medium mixing bowl, mix all of the seasonings. Brush the duck with olive oil and then coat with the seasonings.
3. Put the duck, breast side up, in air fryer basket, air fry at 300°F/150°C for 60 minutes.
4. When time is up, remove from air fryer, let the duck rest for 11 minutes before carving.

Calories: 67kcal, Carbohydrates: 1g, Protein: 1g, Fat: 7g, Fiber: 1g, Sugar: 1g.

CRISPY-SKIN WHOLE CHICKEN WITH HERBS

Serving Size	Prep Time	Cooking time	Total Time
4 Servings	20 Minutes	65 Minutes	85 Minutes

Ingredients

- 2.5kg chicken
- 2 tbsp oil
- 1 tbsp lemon juice
- 1/2 tsp garlic powder
- 1/2 tsp smoked paprika
- 2 tsp dried oregano
- Salt & pepper to taste
- Cooking spray

Directions

1. In small mixing bowl, mix all the seasoning.
2. Brush the chicken with oil. Rub seasoning mixture all over chicken.
3. Spray the air fryer basket with cooking spray.
4. Put chicken breast side down in the the air fryer basket.
5. Air fry at 365°F/185°C for 50 minutes, then flip the chicken to breast side up. Air fry for more 15 minutes.
6. Remove from air fryer. Let rest for 10 minutes. Carve and serve.

calories: 312kcal, carbohydrates: 2g, protein: 42g, fat: 14g, fiber: 1g, sugar: 1g.

TURKEY BURGERS

Serving Size	Prep Time	Cooking time	Total Time
4 Servings	10 Minutes	12 Minutes	22 Minutes

Ingredients

- 450g ground turkey
- 2 cloves garlic, (minced)
- 1 tbsp Worcestershire sauce
- 1 tsp dried oregano
- 1 onion, (minced)
- Salt & pepper to taste
- Cooking spray

Directions

1. Preheat air fryer at 385°F/195°C.
2. In a large mixing bowl, add ground turkey, garlic, Worcestershire sauce, dried oregano, onion, and season with salt & pepper. Mix until just combined.
3. Divide & flatten into 4 patties. Spray both sides with cooking spray.
4. Air Fry for 12 minutes, flipping halfway through cooking time.
5. Serve on buns, topped with your favorite burger toppings.

356kcal, carbohydrates: 30g, protein: 32g, fat: 13g, fiber: 5g, sugar: 4g

"SHAKE 'N BAKE" STYLE CHICKEN

Serving Size	Prep Time	Cooking time	Total Time
4 Servings	5 Minutes	35 Minutes	40 Minutes

Ingredients

- 1 kg chicken drumsticks
- 2 egg, (beaten)
- 200g seasoned breading mix
- Salt & pepper to taste
- Cooking spray

Directions

1. Preheat Air Fryer at 360°F/180°C.
2. In a large mixing bowl, add chicken, beaten egg, and season with salt & pepper. Mix until chicken fully covered with egg mixture. Then coat with the seasoned breading mix.
3. Spray air fryer basket with cooking spray.
4. Put the coated chicken in the air fryer basket in a single layer. Spray the chicken with cooking spray.
5. Air Fry for 35 minutes, flipping halfway through cooking time.
6. Remove from air fryer, serve.

calories: 285kcal, carbohydrates: 5g, protein: 22g, fat: 19g.

ORANGE CHICKEN

Serving Size	Prep Time	Cooking time	Total Time
2 Servings	10 Minutes	10 Minutes	20 Minutes

Ingredients

- 500g boneless skinless chicken breasts or thighs
- 2 tbsp cornstarch
- For the Sauce
- 125ml orange juice
- 2 tbsp brown sugar
- 1 tbsp soy sauce
- 1 tbsp rice vinegar
- 1/2 tsp fresh grated ginger
- zest of one orange
- 2 tsp cornstarch
- 2 tsp water
- Chopped green onions, (garnish)

Directions

1. Preheat air fryer to 400°F/200°C.
2. In a large mixing bowl, add chicken, cornstarch, salt & pepper. Mix until all sides of chicken coated with cornstarch.
3. Spray air fryer basket with cooking spray. Put the chicken in a single layer in the air fryer basket. Spray the top of chicken with cooking spray.
4. Air Fry for for 10 minutes, flipping halfway through cooking time.
5. In a small saucepan over medium heat, add all sauce ingredients. Bring to a boil and simmer for 5 minutes. Stirring continuously.
6. Remove chicken from the air fryer and add it to the sauce. Mix.
7. Top with green onions and serve.

calories: 400kcal, carbohydrates: 26g, protein: 25g, fat: 4g, fiber: 11g, sugar: 15g

DORITOS CRUSTED CHICKEN STRIPS

Serving Size	Prep Time	Cooking time	Total Time
4 Servings	15 Minutes	25 Minutes	40 Minutes

Ingredients

- 255g Doritos, (crushed into small pieces)
- 2 large eggs, (beaten)
- 900g chicken, (thin strips)
- 1 tsp. garlic powder
- Salt & pepper to taste
- Cooking spray

Directions

1. Season the strips with garlic powder, salt & pepper.
2. In a large mixing bowl, put crushed Doritos. In another bowl, put eggs.
3. Coat the strips with the beaten egg, then coat with the crushed Doritos. Press chips into chicken.
4. Preheat air fryer at 380°F/195°C for 5 minutes. Spray air fryer basket with cooking spray. Put chicken strips in the basket in a single layer (you may need to work in batches). Spray cooking spray on top of chicken.
5. Air fry for 15 mins. After 15 mins flip the chicken and spray with cooking spray. Air fry for 5 mins, until crispy & golden brown
6. Serve with favorite dip.

calories: 394kcal, carbohydrates: 28g, protein: 37g, fat: 15g, fiber: 2g, sugar: 1g

HERBED CHICKEN BREAST

Serving Size	Prep Time	Cooking time	Total Time
2 Servings	5 Minutes	18 Minutes	23 Minutes

Ingredients

- 2 (230g each) chicken breasts, (boneless & skinless)
- 2 garlic cloves, (minced)
- 1/2 tsp. dried basil
- 1/2 tsp. dried oregano
- Salt & pepper to taste
- Cooking spray

Directions

1. Coat chicken breasts with oil, then season with garlic, basil, oregano, salt, & pepper.
2. Spray air fryer basket with cooking spray. Put the chicken in air fryer basket in a single layer.
3. Air Fry at 380°F/193°C for 18 minutes, flipping the chicken halfway through cooking time.
4. When time is up, remove from air fryer, allow the chicken to cool for 5 minutes. Slice and serve.

calories: 259kcal, carbohydrates: 1g, protein: 48g, fat: 6g, sugar: 1g.

CHICKEN STRIPS

Serving Size	Prep Time	Cooking time	Total Time
4 Servings	10 Minutes	15 Minutes	25 Minutes

Ingredients

- 450g boneless skinless chicken breast, (cut into same-sized strips)
- 200g breadcrumbs or your favorite breading mix
- 2 eggs
- 1 tsp garlic powder
- 1 tsp smoked paprika
- Salt & pepper to taste
- Cooking spray

Directions

1. Preheat Air Fryer at 380°F/190°C.
2. In a large mixing bowl, add seasonings and chicken strips. Mix until the chicken strips fully coated with the spices.
3. In another large bowl, add breadcrumbs. In another bowl, add the eggs, whisk until smooth.
4. Dip chicken strips in egg, then in breadcrumbs. Press chicken strips into breadcrumbs so that it sticks and coats the chicken.
5. Spray both sides of chicken with cooking spray. Put chicken strips in air fryer basket in a single layer.
6. Air Fry for 15 minutes. Flipping and spraying with cooking spray halfway through cooking time.
7. Remove from air fryer. Serve chicken strips with your favorite dip.

calories: 225kcal, carbohydrates: 12g, protein: 29g, fat: 6g, fiber: 1g, sugar: 1g

CHICKEN PARMESAN

Serving Size	Prep Time	Cooking time	Total Time
4 Servings	12 Minutes	13 Minutes	25 Minutes

Ingredients

- 700g boneless skinless chicken breasts
- 2 large eggs
- 80g breadcrumbs
- 25g grated parmesan cheese
- Cooking spray
- 500ml marinara sauce or tomato sauce
- 120g grated mozzarella cheese
- Salt & pepper to taste

Directions

1. Cut the chicken breasts in half, lengthwise. Pound the chicken breasts into thinner pieces. Season the chicken with salt & pepper.
2. In a medium bowl, add breadcrumbs and Parmesan cheese. Mix. In another bowl, whisk eggs and set aside.
3. Dip each piece of chicken in egg and then dredge it in the breadcrumb mixture. Spray both sides of chicken with cooking spray.
4. Put chicken in single layer in air fryer basket.
5. Air Fry at 365°F/185°C for 8 minutes. Flip and top chicken with marinara sauce and mozzarella cheese.
6. Air fry for another 3 minutes.

calories: 368kcal, carbohydrates: 8g, protein: 52g, fat: 14g, fiber: 2g, sugar: 6g.

STUFFED CHICKEN BREASTS

Serving Size	Prep Time	Cooking time	Total Time
6 Servings	10 Minutes	10 Minutes	20 Minutes

Ingredients

- 2 medium sized chicken breasts
- 120g Provolone Cheese slices
- 80g Beef Bresaola
- 120 Salami
- 1 large egg, (beaten)
- 100g bread crumbs
- 1 tsp Italian Seasoning
- 1 tbsp butter, (melted)
- Cooking spray
- Salt & pepper to taste

Directions

1. Cut chicken breasts in half horizontally through the middle. With meat tenderizer pound the chicken breasts to about 1/2cm thin. Season with salt & pepper.
2. Put 3 provolone slices, 3 salami slices, and 2 Bresaola slices on each chicken breast. Roll the chicken breast and secure with, toothpicks.
3. Preheat air fryer 400°F/205°C for 10 minutes.
4. In a shallow dish, mix breadcrumbs and Italian seasoning.
5. Roll the chicken in the beaten egg and then coat with breadcrumbs.
6. Spray air fryer basket with cooking spray. Put chicken breasts in the basket, brush with butter.
7. Air fry for 10 minutes. Flip, brush with butter and cook another 10 minutes.
8. Remove from the basket and let cool for 5 minutes. Serve.

calories: 450kcal, carbohydrates: 17g, protein: 4g, fat: 20g, fiber: 1g, sugar: 1g.

AIR FRYER TURKEY BREAST

Serving Size	Prep Time	Cooking time	Total Time
10 Servings	5 Minutes	55 Minutes	60 Minutes

Ingredients

- 2k turkey breast, on the bone with skin (ribs removed)
- 1 tbsp olive oil
- 2 tsp salt
- 1 tbsp dried thyme
- 1 tbsp dried rosemary
- 2 tsp dried oregano
- 3 tbsp brown sugar
- 2 tbsp garlic powder
- 2 tsp pepper
- 1 tbsp chili powder
- 2 tsp smoked paprika

Directions

1. Rub 1/2 tbsp of oil all over the turkey breast. Season both sides with salt and seasonings then rub in the remaining half tbsp of oil over the skin side.
2. Preheat the air fryer 350°F/180°C and cook skin side down 20 minutes, turn over and cook until the internal temperature is 160F using an instant-read thermometer about 40 minutes. Let is rest 10 minutes before carving.

Calories: 226kcal, Protein: 32.5g, Fat: 10g, Saturated Fat: 2.5g, Cholesterol: 84mg, Sodium: 296mg

CHICKEN BURGERS

Serving Size	Prep Time	Cooking time	Total Time
4 Servings	5 Minutes	15 Minutes	20 Minutes

Ingredients

- 450g ground chicken
- 3 cloves garlic minced
- salt & pepper to taste
- 1 tbsp worchestershire sauce

Directions

1. In a medium bowl combine chicken, garlic, salt, pepper and worcestershire sauce. Shape into four patties.
2. Add two patties to the air fryer basket and cook at 360°F/182°C for 7 minutes. Flip the patties and continue to cook for 5 minutes until cooked throughout.

calories: 134kcal, carbohydrates: 2g, protein: 27g, fat: 2g

BBQ CHICKEN WINGS

Serving Size	Prep Time	Cooking time	Total Time
10 Servings	10 Minutes	10 Minutes	20 Minutes

Ingredients

- 450g chicken wings
- 1 tbsp oil
- 1 tsp garlic powder
- salt & pepper to taste
- ½ tsp baking powder
- 2 tbsp Scallions for garnish
- 125g bbq sauce

Directions

1. Cut wings into sections (drumettes, wingettes and tips). Discard the tips.
2. Pat chicken dry with paper towel. Drizzle with oil, add salt, pepper, garlic and baking powder. mix to combine.
3. Transfer seasoned wings into air fryer basket. air fry at 400°F / 200°C for 20 mins. flip wings half way through cooking time.
4. Transfer cooked wings into a clean bowl, add the bbq sauce to wings and mix until all well coated in the sauce.
5. put the wings back in the air fryer at 400°F / 200°C for a minute or two then serve.

CHINESE CHICKEN ON A STICK

Serving Size	Prep Time	Cooking time	Total Time
6 Servings	5 Minutes	15 Minutes	20 Minutes

Ingredients

- 600g boneless chicken breasts or thighs, Cut into bite sized cubes
- 2 tsp sesame oil
- 1 tsp garlic powder
- Salt & pepper to taste
- 4 tbsp Oyster sauce
- 2 tbsp sriracha sauce
- 2 tbsp soy sauce

Directions

1. Mix oil oyster sauce and sriracha, divide mixture into two and set one part aside.
2. Add oil, half of the oyster sauce mix, soy sauce, garlic powder black pepper to the chicken, mix till chicken is coated. Thread coated chicken through skewers
3. Place in a lined air Fryer basket and air fry at 400°F / 205°C for 7 mins. After 7 mins brush some sauce in the chicken before flipping them over. cook for 7 mins then brush the last sauce on chicken then cook for 1 min.
4. Serve as is or with your favorite side dishes

calories: 201kcal, carbohydrates: 3g, protein: 22g, fat: 11g, fiber: 1g, sugar: 1g.

LEMON PEPPER CHICKEN

Serving Size	Prep Time	Cooking time	Total Time
4 Servings	10 Minutes	15 Minutes	25 Minutes

Ingredients

- 600g boneless skinless chicken thighs
- 1 tbsp Olive oil (or cooking oil of choice)
- 2½ tsp Lemon pepper seasoning
- 1½ tsp Garlic powder

__Lemon pepper butter sauce__

- 2 tbsp Butter (melted)
- 1½ tsp Lemon pepper seasoning

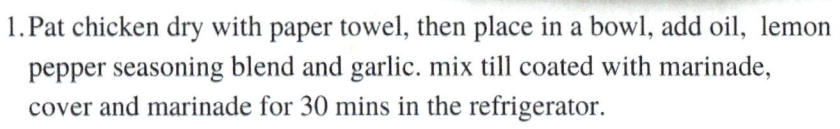

Directions

1. Pat chicken dry with paper towel, then place in a bowl, add oil, lemon pepper seasoning blend and garlic. mix till coated with marinade, cover and marinade for 30 mins in the refrigerator.
2. Place marinated chicken thighs in the air fryer and air fry at 400°F / 200°C for 18 mins. Flipping halfway through.
3. Mix the butter and 1 ½ tsp lemon pepper seasoning.
4. Brush butter and lemon pepper mix all over chicken and serve with your favorite side dish

calories: 205kcal, carbohydrates: 1g, protein: 33g, fat: 7g, fiber: 1g, sugar: 1g.

BBQ CHICKEN LEGS

Serving Size	Prep Time	Cooking time	Total Time
4 Servings	5 Minutes	15 Minutes	20 Minutes

Ingredients

- 8 chicken legs
- 2 tsp smoked paprika
- Salt & pepper to taste
- 80g BBQ saucce

Directions

1. Preheat air fryer at 400°F/205°C.
2. Pat dry chicken legs with paper towels and sprinkle the chicken legs with salt, smoked paprika and pepper.
3. Add the chicken legs to the air fryer basket, four at a time. Cook for 13 minutes. Open the air fryer and flip the chicken legs. Cook for 8 minutes.
4. Open the air fryer and brush each chicken leg with BBQ sauce. Cook for 2 minutes.
5. Repeat this process with the remaining four chicken legs

calories: 596kcal, carbohydrates: 11g, protein: 43g, fat: 41g, fiber: 1g, sugar: 8g.

SMOKY CHICKEN

Serving Size	Prep Time	Cooking time	Total Time
2 Servings	5 Minutes	16 Minutes	21 Minutes

Ingredients

- 2 Chicken Breasts boneless, skinless
- 1 tbsp Smoked Paprika
- 1 tbsp Oregano
- ½ tbsp Garlic Salt
- ¼ tbsp Cinnamon

Directions

1. mix all the spices together and set aside.
2. Gently pat the spice mixture into chicken breasts, flip the chicken breasts and repeat.
3. Place the breasts into the air fryer basket. Spray with cooking spray.
4. Air Fry the breasts at 350°F/175°C for 18 minutes. Flip midway through cooking time and Spray again with cooking spray. Cook until the breasts are at 165°F/73°C. Use a meat thermometer to measure the temp.

calories: 264kcal, carbohydrates: 1g, protein: 48g, fat: 6g, fiber: 1g, sugar: 1g. Sodium: 844mg

TERIYAKI CHICKEN THIGHS

Serving Size	Prep Time	Cooking time	Total Time
8 Servings	10 Minutes	15 Minutes	1H 25 Minutes

Ingredients

- 8 Boneless, Chicken Thighs
- 120g Soy Sauce
- 60ml Water
- 2 tbsp Rice Wine Vinegar
- 2 tbsp Brown Sugar
- 50g Granulated Sugar
- 1 Clove Garlic, minced
- 1 tsp Ground Ginger
- Diced Green Onion

Directions

1. In a small bowl, add soy sauce, water, rice wine vinegar, brown sugar, regular sugar, garlic, and ginger. Whisk until combined.
2. Add chicken thighs into a large Ziploc Bag. Pour soy sauce mixture into bag. Seal the bag and toss it until chicken fully coated, let it sit for at least 60 minutes.
3. Spray air fryer basket with cooking spray, then place the chicken thighs evenly into the air fryer. (in 2 batches) Cook at 390°F/205°C for 10 minutes.
4. Rotate the chicken carefully. Cook for an additional 8 minutes until they reach an internal temperature of 165 degrees.
5. Remove and serve with diced green onions.

calories: 181kcal, carbohydrates: 10g, protein: 23g, fat: 5g, fiber: 1g, sugar: 6g. Sodium: 912mg

CHICKEN PESTO

Serving Size	Prep Time	Cooking time	Total Time
4 Servings	2 Minutes	16 Minutes	18 Minutes

Ingredients

- 120g Basil Pesto Sauce
- 4 Boneless, Skinless Chicken Thighs
- Fresh Mozzarella
- Sliced Roma Tomatoes (Optional)
- Cooking Spray

Directions

1. Add the pesto to a bowl, then coat each chicken thigh in pesto.
2. Spray air fryer basket with cooking spray. Place the chicken evenly in air fryer basket.
3. Air Fry at 390°F/200°C for 18 minutes, flip the chicken halfway through the cooking time and it.
4. Once the chicken is cooked top it with fresh mozzarella & sliced tomatoes and cook for 2 minutes to melt the mozzarella.
5. Serve.

calories: 254kcal, carbohydrates: 2g, protein: 23g, fat: 16g, fiber: 1g, sugar: 1g. Sodium: 390mg

SWEET & SOUR CHICKEN

Serving Size	Total Time	Cooking time	Total Time
4 Servings	13 Minutes	15 Minutes	28 Minutes

Ingredients

<u>Chicken</u>

1 kg boneless skinless chicken breasts, cut into cubes
salt and pepper to taste
125g cornstarch 1 scant cup

<u>Sweet & Sour Sauce</u>

100g granulated sugar
120g ketchup
240g apple cider vinegar
2 tbsp soy sauce
2 tsp garlic salt

Directions

1. Preheat air fryer at 400°F/205°C for 5 minutes.
2. Add the chicken to a Ziploc bag with cornstarch, salt, and pepper. Shake to coat evenly.
3. Spray air fryer basket with cooking spray.
4. Remove chicken from the bag and shake off any excess coating. Add chicken in a single layer in air fryer basket and spray tops with cooking spray.
5. Cook for 8 minutes. Flip at halfway point.
6. Whisk sauce ingredients together in oven safe dish. Add in the chicken and cook for 5 minutes. Chicken will register at 165°F/74°C with an instant read thermometer once it is finished cooking.

Calories: 589kcal | Carbohydrates: 63g | Protein: 61g | Fat: 7g | Sodium: 2058mg | Fiber: 1g | Sugar: 32g

CHICKEN KABOBS

Serving Size	Prep Time	Cooking time	Total Time
4 Servings	10 Minutes	15 Minutes	2 hrs

Ingredients

- 900g skinless chicken thighs or chicken breasts, cut into bite-size cubes
- 120ml Tamari or soy sauce
- 60ml coconut milk
- 3 tbsp lime juice
- 3 tbsp maple syrup
- 1 tbsp Thai red curry

Directions

1. Mix soy sauce, coconut milk, lime juice, honey, and Thai red curry paste in a mixing bowl. Add the chicken and let marinate for at least 2 hours.
2. Soak bamboo skewers for 30 minutes.
3. Thread marinated chicken onto skewers.
4. Preheat Air Fryer to 350°F/175°C. Cook for 15 minutes, turn once halfway through.

calories: 363kcal, carbohydrates: 13g, protein: 47g, fat: 13g, fiber: 1g, sugar: 10g. Sodium: 1825mg

CHICKEN QUESADILLA

Serving Size	Prep Time	Cooking time	Total Time
4 Servings	3 Minutes	10 Minutes	15 Minutes

Ingredients

- 2 corn tortillas
- 3 tbsp guacamole
- 60g cheddar cheese grated
- 100g cooked chicken breast cubed

Directions

1. Preheat air fryer to 325°F/170°C.
2. spray the air fryer basket with cooking spray.
3. add the first tortilla inside the basket. Then spread on the guacamole, add the cheese and chicken and then top with the second tortilla.
4. Use a toothpick to hold the top tortilla in place during cooking.
5. Cook for 6-10 mins, flipping the quesadilla over halfway through.
6. Remove from the air fryer, cut and serve.

calories: 106kcal, carbohydrates: 7g, protein: 7g, fat: 6g, fiber: 2g, sugar: 1g. Sodium: 87mg

BBQ CHICKEN KABOBS

Serving Size	Prep Time	Cooking time	Total Time
4 Servings	7 Minutes	5 Minutes	12 Minutes

Ingredients

- 450g chicken breast, (cut into 5cm pieces)
- 1 red bell pepper, (cut into 5cm pieces)
- 1 red onion, (cut into 5cm pieces)
- 1 tbsp BBQ Sauce
- Salt & pepper to taste

Directions

1. Assemble the kabobs by threading them on the skewer in any order you like.
2. Brush skewers with BBQ sauce, then season with salt & pepper. Put the skewers in the air fryer basket.
3. Air fry 380°F/195°C for 5 minutes on each side.

Calories: 407kca, lCarbohydrates: 9g, Protein: 48g, Fat: 19g, Fiber: 2g, Sugar: 5g.

HONEY GARLIC CHICKEN WINGS

Serving Size	Prep Time	Cooking time	Total Time
6 Servings	15 Minutes	10 Minutes	25 Minutes

Ingredients

- 15 chicken wings, (cut into wings and drummies)
- 100ml olive oil
- 8 garlic cloves, (minced)
- 1 tbsp. granulated sugar
- 1 tbsp. sriracha sauce
- 1 tbsp butter
- 4 tbsp. soy sauce
- 100g honey
- 125ml water
- 1 tsp cornstarch
- 1 tbsp toasted sesame seeds

Directions

1. Preheat the Air Fryer to 370°F/190°C.
2. In a bowl, add chicken and oil, mix until chicken fully coated with oil.
3. Put the wings in a single layer in air fryer basket and air fry for 18 minutes. Flip the wings every 6 minutes.
4. In a medium saucepan over medium high heat, add garlic, sugar, sriracha, butter, soy sauce, honey, water, cornstarch and sesame, and bring to a boil. Reduce heat and simmer for 10 minutes, stirring constantly.
5. When the wings done cooking, transfer them to bowl and cover them with sauce. Serve.

Per Serving: Calories: 558kcal, Carbohydrates: 28g, Protein: 24g, Fat: 40g, Fiber: 1g, Sugar: 25g.

CORNISH HEN

Serving Size	Prep Time	Cooking time	Total Time
4 Servings	15 Minutes	35 Minutes	40 Minutes

Ingredients

- 2 cornish hens, (700g each)
- 2 tbsp olive oil
- 1 1/2 tsp Italian seasoning
- 1 tsp garlic powder
- 1 tsp smoked paprika
- 1 tbsp lemon juice
- Salt & pepper to taste

Directions

1. Preheat your air fryer to 350°F/180°C.
2. Pat dry hens with paper towels. Set aside.
3. In a medium bowl, mix all of the seasonings. Brush the hens with olive oil and then coat with the seasonings.
4. Put the hens, breast side down, in air fryer basket, air fry for 35 minutes. Then flip and air fry for another 10 minutes.
5. When time is up, remove from air fryer, let the hen rest for 11 minutes before carving.

Calories: 350kcal, Carbohydrates: 1g, Protein: 26g, Fat: 18g, Fiber: 1g, Sugar: 0g

CHICKEN DRUMSTICKS

Serving Size	Prep Time	Cooking time	Total Time
4 Servings	5 Minutes	20 Minutes	25 Minutes

Ingredients

- 4 chicken drumsticks
- 1 tbsp olive oil
- 2 tbsp plain flour
- 1 tsp baking soda
- 1 tsp paprika
- ½ tsp onion powder
- Salt & pepper to taste
- Cooking spray

Directions

1. Brush drumsticks with oil and then put into a Ziploc bag.
2. In a small mixing bowl, add flour, baking soda, paprika, onion powder, and season with salt & pepper. Mix until combined.
3. Add flour mixture into the Ziploc bag with chicken and toss until the drumsticks are coated with the flour mixture.
4. Spray the air fryer basket with cooking spray. Put the drumsticks in air fryer basket in a single layer.
5. Air fry at 400°F/205°C for 23 minutes. Flipping halfway through the cooking time.
6. When time is up, remove from air fryer, Then serve.

Calories: 167kcal, Carbohydrates: 3g, Protein: 14g, Fat: 11g, Fiber: 1g, Sugar: 1g.

48

CHICKEN STREET TACOS

Serving Size	Prep Time	Cooking time	Total Time
18 Servings	10 Minutes	10 Minutes	20 Minutes

Ingredients

- 500g chicken breast, (cut into strips)
- 2 tsp chili powder
- Salt & pepper to taste
- Cooking spray
- 12 flour tortillas (10cm in size)

Directions

1. Spray the air fryer basket with cooking spray.
2. In a medium mixing bowl, add chicken, chili powder, and season with salt & pepper. Mix until well coated with the seasonings.
3. Put the chicken into the air fryer basket
4. Air fry at 380°F/195°C for 10 minutes, flipping halfway through cooking time.
5. Serve over taco tortillas.

Calories: 362kcal, Carbohydrates: 34g, Protein: 30g, Fat: 11g, Fiber: 2g, Sugar: 3g

CHICKEN NUGGETS

Serving Size	Prep Time	Cooking time	Total Time
4 Servings	10 Minutes	15 Minutes	25 Minutes

Ingredients

- 600g chicken breasts, (cut into bite-size pieces)
- 1 tbsp oil

Wet Batter
- 120ml cold water
- 1 large egg
- 90g plain flour

Coating
- 100g breadcrumbs
- 1/4 tsp cayenne pepper
- 1/4 tsp garlic powder
- Salt & pepper to taste

Directions

1. Preheat air fryer at 430°F/220°C for 10 minutes.
2. In a large bowl, add flour. In another bowl, add egg and water, whisk them. Sift in the flour a few tbsp at a time, until a thick batter is formed. In a third bowl, add breadcrumbs and the seasonings.
3. Dip each chicken piece into the flour, then wet batter and then into the breadcrumbs.
4. Spray the air fryer basket with cooking spray. Put chicken pieces in the air fryer basket and spread them into a single layer. Spray chicken with cooking spray.
5. Air Fry at 360°F/180°C for 11 minutes, Flipping and spraying them with cooking spray halfway through cooking time.

calories: 430kcal, carbohydrates: 25g, protein: 30g, fat: 8g, fiber: 2g, sugar: 2g.

GARLIC PARMESAN CHICKEN BITES

Serving Size	Prep Time	Cooking time	Total Time
4 Servings	5 Minutes	18 Minutes	23 Minutes

Ingredients

- 700g boneless skinless chicken breasts, (cut into about 2.5cm pieces)
- 2 tsp oil
- 1 tbsp Worcestershire sauce
- 1/2 tsp dried oregano
- 1 tsp garlic powder
- 1/2 tsp onion powder
- 2 tbsp plain flour
- 3 tbsp grated Parmesan cheese
- Salt & pepper to taste

Directions

1. In a large bowl, add chicken, oil, Worcestershire sauce, oregano, garlic, onion powder, Season with salt & pepper.
2. Spray the air fryer basket with cooking spray. Add chicken and spread into single layer.
3. Air Fry at 360°F/180°C for 18 minutes. Flipping chicken halfway through cooking time.
4. Add Parmesan cheese, then Air Fry for 1 minute. Serve warm.

calories: 258kcal, carbohydrates: 5g, protein: 38g, fat: 9g, fiber: 1g, sugar: 1g.

TURKEY MEATBALLS

Serving Size	Prep Time	Cooking time	Total Time
4 Servings	10 Minutes	10 Minutes	15 Minutes

Ingredients

- 680g ground turkey
- 1 red bell pepper red, (chopped)
- 30g parsley, (chopped)
- 1 egg
- 1 tbsp. Italian seasoning
- Salt & pepper to taste

Directions

1. Preheat the Air Fryer to 400°F/205°C.
2. In a large mixing bowl, add all ingredients. Mix until all combined.
3. Use a tbsp to shape meatballs into 1.5 inch/3cm each balls.
4. Put the meatballs in the air fryer basket in a single layer (you may need to work in batches).
5. Air fry for 10 minutes, until cooked through.
6. Remove from the air fryer and Serve.

Calories: 149kcal, Carbohydrates: 2g, Protein: 28g, Fat: 3g, Fiber: 1g, Sugar: 1g.

KIELBASA VEGGIE

Serving Size	Prep Time	Cooking time	Total Time
4 Servings	10 Minutes	14 Minutes	24 Minutes

Ingredients

- 400g turkey kielbasa cut on the diagonal into 1/2-inch/1.5cm thick slices
- 225g asparagus trimmed, cut into 2-inch/5cm pieces
- 200g zucchini, cut into 2-inch/5cm slices
- ½ tbsp avocado oil
- salt & pepper to taste
- ¾ tsp Italian seasoning
- 1 tsp paprika
- ½ tsp garlic powder

Directions

1. Combine asparagus, peppers, and kielbasa in a bowl, and stir in oil.
2. Blend sea salt, Italian seasoning, paprika, garlic powder, and black pepper together.
3. Add seasonings into the asparagus, peppers, and kielbasa mixture.
4. Pour the mixture in the air fryer basket and cook at 380°F/193°C for 12 minutes, stirring half way through cooking. Add tomatoes and cook for 2 minutes more if desired.
5. Remove from the air fryer basket and serve.

Serving: 1.5cup | Calories: 210kcal | Carbohydrates: 7g | Protein: 20g | Fat: 11g | Sodium: 940mg | Fiber: 3g | Sugar: 3g

RAMEN NOODLE STIR

Serving Size	Prep Time	Cooking time	Total Time
2 Servings	5 Minutes	8 Minutes	13 Minutes

Ingredients

- 85g Ramen Noodles
- ¼ package frozen Stir fry Vegetable mix
- 90g precooked chicken breast strips

Directions

1. Boil water and cook ramen noodles according to its package directions.
2. Place frozen vegetables and frozen (or cold) chicken in the air fryer basket.
3. Season the vegetables and chicken.
4. Cook at 370°F/188°C for 8 minutes until vegetables and chicken are warmed through and crispy to your liking.
5. combine the noodles with the vegetables and chicken. Add any additional seasonings or sauces and enjoy!

Calories: 424kcal | Carbohydrates: 50g | Protein: 34g | Fat: 10g | Sodium: 1077mg | Fiber: 8g | Sugar: 1g

RANCH CHICKEN AND VEGGIES

Serving Size	Prep Time	Cooking time	Total Time
4 Servings	15 Minutes	23 Minutes	30 Minutes

Ingredients

- 450g chicken, cut into bite size pieces
- 2 tbsp honey
- 2 tbsp Worcestershire sauce
- 3 tbsp ranch dressing mix divided
- 2 tbsp oil divided
- 450g potato, cut into bite size pieces
- 1 zucchini cut into bite size pieces
- 1 Onion cut into bite size pieces
- ½ tsp pepper

Directions

1. Mix honey, Worcestershire sauce, 2 tbsp Ranch Dressing Mix, and 1 tbsp oil. add chicken into marinade and let it marinade for 30 minutes.
2. in a large bowl, add potato, zucchini and onion, add 1 tbsp oil then season with 1 tbsp of Ranch Dressing. Season with pepper. mix.
3. Cook the veggies first at 350°F/175°C for 15 minutes. Then, top veggies with chicken and cook for 8 minutes.

Calories: 350kcal | Carbohydrates: 39g | Protein: 13g | Fat: 15g | Sodium: 1004mg | Fiber: 3g | Sugar: 12g

SPICY APRICOT CHICKEN

Serving Size	Prep Time	Cooking time	Total Time
4 Servings	7 Minutes	10 Minutes	17 Minutes

Ingredients

- 100g apricot preserves
- 60g chili sauce
- 1 tbsp hot mustard
- ¼ tsp salt
- ⅛ tsp pepper
- 4 boneless skinless chicken breast halves 4 ounces/115g each

Directions

1. In a medium saucepan over medium-low heat, combine the apricot preserves, chili sauce, and hot mustard. Stir and heat.
2. Pound the thicker end of each chicken breast to even it out. Pat chicken dry with a paper towel. Spray chicken with oil and rub to coat. Sprinkle with salt and pepper. Place the chicken in the air fryer basket.
3. Cook at 380°F/193°C for 10 minutes. At the halfway point, flip the chicken and brush on some sauce onto the chicken breasts. Continue cooking until an instant read thermometer inserted into the center of the thickest part of the chicken reads 155°F/68°C.
4. Let chicken rest for 10 minutes, then slice and serve.

Calories: 197kcal | Carbohydrates: 16g | Protein: 25g | Fat: 3g | Sodium: 555mg | Fiber: 1g | Sugar: 10g

HONEY MUSTARD CHICKEN BREASTS

Serving Size	Prep Time	Cooking time	Total Time
6 Servings	15 Minutes	12 Minutes	27 Minutes

Ingredients

- 2 tbsp butter
- 85g honey
- 60g dijon mustard
- 1 tbsp oil
- 2 tsp fresh lemon juice
- salt & pepper to taste
- 4 boneless skinless chicken breasts

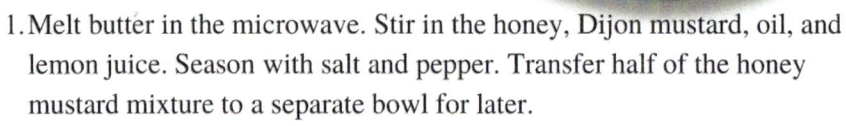

Directions

1. Melt butter in the microwave. Stir in the honey, Dijon mustard, oil, and lemon juice. Season with salt and pepper. Transfer half of the honey mustard mixture to a separate bowl for later.
2. Pound down the chicken about 1 inch/2.5cm thick. Brush both sides of the chicken with honey mustard and place it in sprayed air fryer basket.
3. Cook at 380°F/193°C for 12 minutes, flipping halfway through cooking time. serve with remaining sauce.

Calories: 190kcal | Carbohydrates: 12g | Protein: 17g | Fat: 8g | Sodium: 239mg | Fiber: 1g | Sugar: 12g

ROASTED CHICKEN SAUSAGE AND VEGGIES

Serving Size	Prep Time	Cooking time	Total Time
6 Servings	5 Minutes	20 Minutes	25 Minutes

Ingredients

- 340g package chicken sausage cut into 2-inch/5cm slices
- 250g bell pepper, sliced
- 2 tbsp oil
- 1 large onion, sliced
- zest of 1 lemon
- 4 cloves garlic minced
- 1 tbsp fresh parsley minced
- salt & pepper to taste

Directions

1. Toss the sausage, onion and bell pepper in a bowl
2. Stir in oil, lemon zest, garlic, parsley, salt, and pepper to evenly coat the sausage and veggie mixture.
3. Place in the air fryer and cook at 380°F/187°C for 13 minutes, stirring halfway. Cook until veggies reach desired tenderness.

Calories: 267kcal | Carbohydrates: 28g | Protein: 13g | Fat: 13g | Sodium: 1029mg | Fiber: 6g | Sugar: 7g

CHICKEN EMPANADAS

Serving Size	Prep Time	Cooking time	Total Time
24 Servings	35 Minutes	10 Minutes	45 Minutes

Ingredients

- 24 Empanada Discs
- 500g Ground chicken
- 1 tbsp. Olive Oil
- 1 Onion, chopped
- 1 Garlic Clove, chopped
- 2 tsp. Cumin Powder
- 2 tsp. Fresh Oregano
- 1 cup Green Olives, pitted and halved
- 30g Capers
- 30g Parsley, chopped
- Salt & Pepper to taste
- 1 Egg, for the egg wash

Directions

1. in s skillet to medium-high, add oil, onion, garlic clove, cumin powder, and fresh oregano. Cook for 15 minutes until onion is soft. Add green olives and capers, cook for 3 minutes .
2. Add ground chicken and break it up, cook for 10 minutes until completely browned. Season with salt & pepper.
3. Fill the empanada disks with 1 tbsp. of chicken and seal them using a fork. Brush them with egg wash.
4. pray Air fryer basket with cooking spray. Cook 350°F/180°C in batches.
5. Serve the empanadas with the salsa verde

Calories: 168kcal | Carbohydrates: 15g | Protein: 7g | Fat: 2g | Fiber: 2g |

PIZZA STUFFED CHICKEN THIGHS

Serving Size	Prep Time	Cooking time	Total Time
8 Servings	12 Minutes	14 Minutes	26 Minutes

Ingredients

- 4-5 boneless skinless chicken thighs
- 125g pizza sauce
- 14 slices turkey pepperoni
- ½ small red onion sliced
- 145g sliced mozzarella cheese
- 60g shredded cheese for topping mozzarella, parmesan, Italian blend, any cheese that you love!

Directions

1. Place chicken thighs flat in between two pieces of parchment paper. Pound the chicken to create a thin piece.
2. Spread a spoonful of pizza sauce on each piece of chicken. Add cheese, 2-4 pieces of pepperoni, and onion slices on top.
3. Fold one side of the chicken over onto the other and hold the chicken together with a toothpick or skewer.
4. Preheat the air fryer at 400°F/205°C for 5 minutes.
5. Place parchment paper in the air fryer basket and set chicken in air fryer, cook at 370°F/190°C for 12 minutes.
6. Add cheese on the top of the chicken for the 2 minutes.

Calories: 155kcal | Carbohydrates: 2g | Protein: 18g | Fat: 8g | Sodium: 343mg | Fiber: 1g | Sugar: 1g

CHICKEN THIGHS

Serving Size	Prep Time	Cooking time	Total Time
8 Servings	5 Minutes	12 Minutes	17 Minutes

Ingredients

- 900g boneless skinless chicken thighs
- 2 tsps avocado oil or other oil
- 2 tsps chili powder
- 1 tsp cumin
- 1 tsp garlic powder
- 1 tsp salt
- ½ tsp pepper
- Pinch cayenne pepper

Directions

1. In a small bowl, add chili powder, cumin, garlic powder, salt, pepper, and cayenne. mix.
2. Pat chicken dry with paper towels, rub with oil, and sprinkle with spice mixture on both sides.
3. Place chicken in air fryer basket and cook at 400°F/204°C for 16 minutes. Flip halfway through cooking.
4. Let chicken cool slightly, then chop into bite-size pieces. Serve chicken with lime wedges over salad.

Calories: 149kcal | Carbohydrates: 1g | Protein: 22g | Fat: 6g | Sodium: 400mg | Fiber: 1g | Sugar: 1g

BEEF & CHEESE QUESADILLA

Serving Size	Prep Time	Cooking time	Total Time
1 Servings	4 Minutes	6 Minutes	10 Minutes

Ingredients

- 2 tortillas
- 2-3 beef slices or protein of your choice
- 45g Monterey jack cheese, or Mozzarella cheese
- Cooking spray

Directions

1. Spray the air fryer basket.
2. Place the tortilla in the air fryer basket. Add beef, cheese, then another tortilla. Spray with oil.
3. Keep the quesadilla down with an air fryer wire rack or tooth picks.
4. Air fry at 360°F/182°C for 6 minutes until the tortilla is crispy.

Calories: 435kcal | Carbohydrates: 30g | Protein: 24g | Fat: 24g | Sodium: 1291mg | Fiber: 2g |

JUICY STEAK AND MUSHROOMS BITES

Serving Size	Prep Time	Cooking time	Total Time
4 Servings	15 Minutes	6 Minutes	2 hours 21 minutes

Ingredients

- 450g steak cut into 1" cubes, pat dry
- 240g mushrooms chopped
- ½ onion sliced

Marinade

- 140g Worcestershire sauce
- ½ tbsp garlic powder
- salt and pepper to taste

Directions

1. Combine the steak, mushrooms, and onions in a bowl with the marinade ingredients. Mix until everything is combined.
2. Cover and marinate for at least 2 hours.
3. Preheat the air fryer at 400°F/205°C for 5 minutes.
4. Air fry at 400°F/205°C for 8 minutes.

Calories: 284kcal | Carbohydrates: 11g | Protein: 25g | Fat: 16g | Sodium: 400mg | Fiber: 1g | Sugar: 5g

GROUND BEEF WELLINGTON

Serving Size	Prep Time	Cooking time	Total Time
2 Servings	30 Minutes	20 Minutes	50 Minutes

Ingredients

- 1 tbsp butter
- 40g chopped fresh mushrooms
- 2 tsp all-purpose flour
- 120g heavy cream
- 1 large egg yolk
- 2 tbsp finely chopped onion
- salt & pepper to taste
- 220g ground beef
- 1 tube (120g) refrigerated crescent rolls
- 1 large egg, lightly beaten,

Directions

1. Preheat air fryer to 300°F/150°C. In a saucepan over medium-high heat, heat butter. Add mushrooms cook for 6 minutes. Stir in flour and pepper until blended. Gradually add cream. Bring to a boil; cook for 2 minutes until thickened. Remove from the heat and set aside.
2. In a bowl, combine egg yolk, onion, 2 tbsp mushroom sauce, salt and pepper. Crumble beef over mixture and mix well. Shape into 2 loaves. Unroll crescent dough and separate into 2 rectangles; press perforations to seal. Place meat loaf on each rectangle. Bring edges together and pinch to seal. brush with beaten egg.
3. Place Wellingtons in a single layer on greased tray in air fryer basket. Cook for 22 minutes until golden brown.
4. warm remaining mushrooms sauce. Serve sauce with Wellingtons.

Calories: 585kcal | Carbohydrates: 30g | Protein: 29g | Fat: 1g | Sodium: 865mg | Fiber: 2g |

STUFFED MEAT LOAF SLICES

Serving Size	Prep Time	Cooking time	Total Time
6 Servings	30 Minutes	15 Minutes	45 Minutes

Ingredients

Filling:

- 420g mashed potatoes (with milk and butter)
- 2 hard-boiled large eggs, chopped
- 140g mayonnaise
- 50g grated Parmesan cheese
- 225g chopped celery
- 1 green onion, chopped
- Salt & pepper to taste
- 1/4 tsp ground mustard

Meat loaf:

- 1 large egg, lightly beaten
- 25g dry bread crumbs
- 1 tsp salt
- 600g ground beef

Directions

1. For filling, mix filling ingredients.
2. In a large bowl, add beaten egg, bread crumbs and salt. Add beef; mix. On a large piece of foil, pat mixture into a 14x8-in/35x20-cm. rectangle. Spread filling over top to within 1-in/2.5cm. of edges. Roll up, starting with a short side, removing foil as you roll. Seal ends; place on a large plate. Refrigerate, covered, overnight.
3. Preheat air fryer to 325°F/162°C. Cut roll into 6 slices. In batches, place slices on greased tray in air fryer basket. Cook for 15 minutes.

Calories: 439kcal | Carbohydrates: 20g | Protein: 24g | Fat: 28g | Sodium: 1187mg | Fiber: 1g | Sugar: 5g

PAPAS RELLENAS

Serving Size	Prep Time	Cooking time	Total Time
2 Servings	45 Minutes	15 Minutes	60 Minutes

Ingredients

- 700g potatoes, peeled and cut into wedges
- 450g ground beef
- 1 small green pepper, finely chopped
- 1 small onion, finely chopped
- 140g tomato sauce
- 65g sliced olives
- 80g raisins
- Salt & pepper to taste
- 1/2 tsp paprika
- 1 tsp garlic powder
- 2 large eggs, lightly beaten
- 60g seasoned bread crumbs

Directions

1. Place potatoes in a large saucepan and cover with water. Bring to a boil. Reduce heat; cover and cook for 17 minutes.
2. in a large skillet over medium heat, cook beef, green pepper and onion until meat is no longer pink; drain. Stir in tomato sauce, olives, raisins, salt, pepper and paprika; heat through.
3. Drain potatoes; mash with garlic powder and salt and pepper. Shape 2 tbsp potatoes into a patty; place a heaping tbsp of filling in the center. Shape potatoes around filling, forming a ball. Repeat.
4. Place eggs and bread crumbs in separate shallow bowls. Dip potato balls in eggs, then roll in bread crumbs. Preheat air fryer to 400°F/205°C. In batches, place in single layer on greased tray in air-fryer basket; spray with cooking spray. Cook for 14 minutes until golden brown.

Calories: 625kcal | Carbohydrates: 40g | Protein: 13g | Fat: 5g | Sodium: 642mg | Fiber: 2g

QUICK TATER TOTS BAKE

Serving Size	Prep Time	Cooking time	Total Time
4 Servings	15 Minutes	30 Minutes	45 Minutes

Ingredients

- 400g pound ground beef or turkey
- 1 small onion, chopped
- Salt and pepper to taste
- 1 package (480g) frozen Tater Tots
- 1 can (300g) condensed cream of mushroom soup, undiluted
- 160ml milk or water
- 65g shredded cheddar cheese

Directions

1. Preheat air fryer to 350°F/180°C. In a large skillet over medium heat, cook beef and onion until meat is no longer pink; drain. Season with salt & pepper.
2. Transfer to a greased baking dish that will fit in the air fryer basket. Top with Tater Tots. Combine soup and milk; pour over potatoes. Sprinkle with cheese. Place baking dish on tray in air-fryer basket. Cook, uncovered 40 minutes.

Calories: 570kcal | Carbohydrates: 37g | Protein: 26g | Fat: 12g | Sodium: 1187mg | Fiber: 4g | Sugar: 5g

BEEF WELLINGTON WONTONS

Serving Size	Prep Time	Cooking time	Total Time
4 Servings	35 Minutes	10 Minutes	45 Minutes

Ingredients

- 225g lean ground beef
- 1 tbsp butter
- 1 tbsp olive oil
- 2 garlic cloves, minced
- 1 tsp chopped shallot
- 120g chopped fresh shiitake
- 120g chopped fresh baby portobello
- 120g chopped fresh white mushrooms
- 1 tbsp minced fresh parsley
- Salt and pepper to taste
- 1 package (360g) wonton wrappers
- 1 large egg
- 1 tbsp water

Directions

1. Preheat air fryer to 325°F/165°C.
2. In a small skillet over medium heat, cook beef for 5 minutes until no longer pink. Transfer to a large bowl. In the same skillet, heat butter and olive oil. Add garlic and shallot; cook 1 minute. Stir in mushrooms. Cook until mushrooms are tender; add to beef. Stir in parsley, salt and pepper.
3. Place about 2 tsp filling in the center of each wonton wrapper. Combine egg and water. Moisten wonton edges with egg mixture; fold opposite corners over filling and press to seal.
4. In batches, arrange wontons in a single layer on greased tray in air-fryer basket; spraywith cooking spray. Cook for 5 minutes. flip and spray with cooking spray. Cook for 5 minutes until golden brown and crisp.

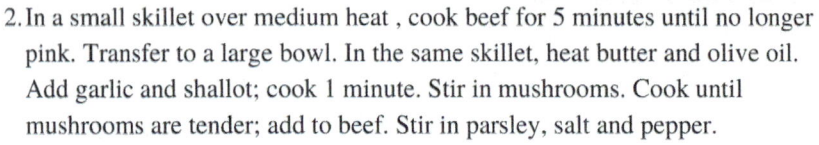

Calories: 42kcal | Carbohydrates: 5g | Protein: 2g | Fat: 5g | Sodium: 82mg

MONGOLIAN BEEF

Serving Size	Prep Time	Cooking time	Total Time
4 Servings	10 Minutes	10 Minutes	20 Minutes

Ingredients

- 450g flank steak, Sliced into thin strips
- 25g cornstarch
- 2 tbsp olive oil
- 4 cloves minced garlic
- 1 tbsp minced ginger
- 120ml low sodium soy sauce
- 120g water
- 100g brown sugar
- 2 green onions, chopped

Directions

1. place beef into a large bowl. Add the cornstarch to the steak and toss to coat. Let set in the cornstarch for 5 minutes.
2. Heat the air fryer to 400°F/205°C.
3. Add the steak to the air fryer basket and spray with cooking spray. Air fry for 10 minutes, shaking the basket & spraying with more cooking spray halfway through cooking.
4. heat oil in a large deep skillet. Add the garlic and ginger and for 30 seconds. Add soy sauce, water, and brown sugar and stir. Bring to a boil and cook for 7 minutes, stirring occasionally, until sauce thickened.
5. Carefully add the cooked beef to the sauce and continue cooking for 2 minutes.
6. Sprinkle chopped green onions over the top before serving.

Calories: 423kcal | Carbohydrates: 33g | Protein: 35g | Fat: 16g | Sodium: 1187mg | Fiber: 1g | Sugar: 23g

KOREAN BBQ BEEF

Serving Size	Prep Time	Cooking time	Total Time
6 Servings	15 Minutes	30 Minutes	45 Minutes

Ingredients

- 450g Flank Steak or Thinly Sliced Steak
- 125g Corn Starch
- Cooking Spray

Sauce

- 110g Soy Sauce
- 100g Brown Sugar
- 2 Tbsp White Wine Vinegar
- 1 Clove Garlic Crushed
- 1 Tbsp Hot Chili Sauce
- 1 Tsp Ground Ginger
- 1 Tbsp Cornstarch
- 1 Tbsp Water

Directions

1. toss sliced steak in the cornstarch.
2. Spray air fryer basket with cooking spray. Add the steak and spray another coat of spray on top.
3. Cook at 390°F/205°C for 10 minutes, turn the steak and cook for 10 minutes.
4. add the sauce ingredients (except the cornstarch and water) to a medium saucepan. bring to a low boil, then whisk in the cornstarch and water.
5. Carefully remove steak and pour sauce over the steak, mix.
6. Serve with cooked rice or fries.

Calories: 487kcal | Carbohydrates: 32g | Protein: 39g | Fat: 22g | Sodium: 1531Mg .Sugar: 21g

KOFTA KEBABS

Serving Size	Prep Time	Cooking time	Total Time
8 Servings	15 Minutes	12 Minutes	30 Minutes

Ingredients

- 450g ground beef
- 450g ground lamb
- 1 small onion, diced finely
- 2 garlic cloves, minced
- 1/4 cup fresh parsley, chopped
- 2 tsp cumin
- salt & pepper to taste
- 1 tsp allspice
- 1/2 tsp nutmeg
- 1/2 tsp paprika
- 1/4 tsp cinnamon

Directions

1. Add all the ingredients to a food processor and pulse until smooth.
2. Divide the meat mixture into even sections & shape into kebabs-like patties.
3. Add kofta kebabs to the air fryer basket. Do not overlap. You may need to cook in batches.
4. Cook at 380°F/195°C for 12 minutes, turning halfway through.

Calories: 238kcal | Carbohydrates: 2g | Protein: 22g | Fat: 115g | Sodium: 509mg | Fiber: 1g | Sugar: 1g

EMPANADAS

Serving Size	Prep Time	Cooking time	Total Time
6 Servings	12 Minutes	10 Minutes	22 Minutes

Ingredients

- 450g ground beef
- 1 red bell pepper diced, or green bell pepper
- 1 medium white onion diced, or yellow onion
- 1 tsp cumin
- 1 tsp oregano
- 1/2 tsp salt
- 1/2 tsp paprika
- 1/2 tsp garlic minced
- 400g pre-made pie crust

Directions

1. In a medium skillet over medium high heat, brown ground beef until nearly cooked, then add pepper and onion. Cook for 5 minutes. Add seasonings and garlic and cook 2 minutes. Remove from heat and let cool.
2. Preheat your air fryer to 390°F/200°C.
3. Roll pie crust dough into a log and cut into 6 equal portions. Roll each portion into a disc about 1/8-inch/0.5cm thick. Fill half of the disc with the cooled filling, folding over the other side of the disc and sealing with a fork around the edge.
4. Spray air fryer with cooking spray. Spray the top of the empanadas and air fry for 8 minutes.

Calories: 399kcal | Carbohydrates: 23g | Protein: 16g | Fat: 26g | Sodium: 420Mg .Sugar: 1g | Fiber: 2g

CHEESE STUFFED MEATBALLS

Serving Size	Prep Time	Cooking time	Total Time
6 Servings	10 Minutes	10 Minutes	20 Minutes

Ingredients

- 450g ground beef
- 1 egg large
- 30g bread crumbs
- 30g parmesan cheese grated
- 2 cloves garlic minced
- 1 tsp Italian seasoning
- 1 tsp paprika
- Salt & pepper to taste
- 25g chopped parsley
- 3 tbs milk
- 100g mozzarella cheese, cut into 18 cubes

Directions

1. In a large bowl, add meat, egg, bread crumbs, parmesan cheese, salt, pepper, garlic, Italian seasoning, paprika, parsley, milk, and mix until combined.
2. Scoop the meat mixture using a cookie dough scoop (18 balls) and place in a baking sheet.
3. flatten the meatball and place the cheese in the middle and shape it into a ball covering the cheese.
4. Preheat Air fryer 370°F/190°C.spray Air fryer basket with cooking spray and place the meatballs on it.
5. Air fry 12 minutes until browned flipping halfway. Remove and cook the next batch.
6. Once all cooked, serve or you can put all together to warm in marinara sauce.

Calories: 305kcal | Carbohydrates: 8g | Protein: 20g | Fat: 121g | Sodium: 287mg | Fiber: 1g | Sugar: 1g

STEAK BITES

Serving Size	Prep Time	Cooking time	Total Time
4 Servings	7 Minutes	8 Minutes	18 Minutes

Ingredients

- 1 kg sirloin steak, (cut into 5cm pieces)
- 2 tbsp oil
- 1 tsp. garlic powder
- 2 tbsp. Worcestershire Sauce
- Salt & pepper to taste

Directions

1. In a large mixing bowl, add steak pieces, add the salt, pepper, garlic powder, oil and Worcestershire sauce. Mix.
2. Cover and refrigerate for at least 30 minutes.
3. Preheat air fryer by setting the temperature to 400°F/205°C for 5 minutes.
4. Coat air fryer basket with cooking spray. Add steak pieces into the hot basket.
5. Air fry for 3 minutes, then flip and air fry for another 3 minutes.
6. Remove from air fryer, serve

480kcal, Fat: 14g, Carbohydrates: 2g, Protein:30g

FLANK STEAK

Serving Size	Prep Time	Cooking time	Total Time
4 Servings	30 Minutes	12 Minutes	42 Minutes

Ingredients

- 850g Flank Steak
- 1 tbsp Olive Oil
- 1 Lime, juiced
- 2 tbsp Orange Juice
- 2 tbsp Soy Sauce
- 3 cloves Garlic, minced
- 1/2 tsp Oregano
- 1 tsp Chili Powder
- 1/2 tsp Cumin
- Salt & pepper to taste

Directions

1. Place the flank steak In a sealable bag and set it aside.
2. In a bowl, combine the rest of the ingredients and whisk until combined. Pour the marinade into the bag with the flank steak. Seal tightly removing any excess air. Store in the refrigerator and marinate for at least 20 minutes.
3. Drain the steak from marinade and discard marinade.
4. Preheat air fryer 400°F/205°C. Add steak to the basket and cook for 7 minutes on each side flipping once.Cook until the internal temperature reads 140-145° Fahrenheit or 130° Farhenheit for medium-rare. Let rest 5 minutes before slicing.
5. Thinly slice steak against the grain. serve in tacos, burritos, nachos, or salads.

Calories: 630kcal | Carbohydrates: 5g | Protein: 50g |
Fat: 15g | Sodium: 1314mg | Fiber: 4g | Sugar: 1g

SAUSAGE BALLS

Serving Size	Prep Time	Cooking time	Total Time
26 BALLS	10 Minutes	8 Minutes	18 Minutes

Ingredients

- 450g Breakfast Sausage
- 240g Pancake Mix
- 1 tsp garlic powder
- 60ml Milk
- 80g Shredded Cheddar Cheese

Directions

1. in a large mixing bowl., mix the breakfast sausage, pancake Mix, garlic powder, milk and cheese.
2. Using a cookie scoop, scoop the dough into balls. Roll and place on a plate.
3. Line air fryer basket or spray with cooking spray, then place them with enough space to cook evenly.
4. Cook at 360°F/182°C 10 minutes until the internal temperature reaches at least 165°F.
5. remove and place on a cooling rack and repeat for remaining batches.

Calories: 88kcal | Carbohydrates: 3g | Protein: 5g | Fat: 6g | Fiber: 1g | Sodium: 202mg .

CORNED BEEF

Serving Size	Prep Time	Cooking time	Total Time
8 Servings	5 Minutes	1H 40Minutes	1H 45 Minutes

Ingredients

- 2 kg corned beef
- salt & pepper to taste
- 1 tsp mustard seeds
- 2 bay leaves, crumbled
- 1/2 tsp ground ginger

Directions

1. Preheat an air fryer to 360°F/182°C .
2. Rinse corned beef under running watere, then pat dry with paper towels. rub with spices.
3. Wrap the corned beef in aluminum foil and place it inside the air fryer basket.
4. Air fry for 1 hour, then open the basket, open the foil, and baste the brisket with juices from the meat.
5. Close and cook for another 40 minutes (until the internal temperature reaches at least 145°F/63°C).
6. open the foil and air fry for 5 minutes.
7. Remove from the air fryer basket and allow to rest for 20 minutes before slicing.

Calories: 494kcal | Carbohydrates: 1g | Protein: 37g | Fat: 135g | Sodium: 3036mg

MEATLOAF

Serving Size	Prep Time	Cooking time	Total Time
4 Servings	7 Minutes	18 Minutes	25 Minutes

Ingredients

- 700g ground beef
- 120g breadcrumbs
- 1 large egg
- 150ml milk
- 1 small onion, (chopped)
- 1 garlic clove, (minced)
- Salt & pepper to taste

Meatloaf Sauce

- 120g ketchup
- 2 tbsp brown sugar
- 1 tsp mustard
- 1 tsp Worcestershire Sauce

Directions

1. In a large mixing bowl, add ground beef, breadcrumbs, egg, milk, onion, and season with salt & pepper. Mix until combined.
2. Shape the meat mixture into a loaf and put it on top of a piece of parchment paper in the air fryer basket.
3. Air fry at 380°F/195°C for 18 minutes.
4. In a small mixing bowl, add ketchup, sugar, mustard and Worcestershire Sauce. Mix together until combined.
5. Once meatloaf done cooking, brush sauce on top.
6. Air fry for an additional 3 minutes.

Calories: 647kcal, Carbohydrates: 37g, Protein: 36g, Fat: 38g, Fiber: 2g, Sugar: 17g

ROSEMARY GARLIC LAMB CHOPS

Serving Size	Prep Time	Cooking time	Total Time
2 Servings	5 Minutes	15 Minutes	20 Minutes

Ingredients

- 600g rack of lamb , about 7-8 chops
- 3 tbsp olive oil
- 2 tbsp chopped fresh rosemary
- 1 tsp garlic powder
- Salt & pepper to taste

Directions

1. Pat dry the lamb rack. Cut into individual chops.
2. In a large bowl, add oil, rosemary, garlic, season with salt, & pepper. Add the lamb chops and mix to coat with seasoning. Cover and refrigerate for 1 hour.
3. Preheat the air fryer at 380°F/195°C for 4 minutes. Spray air fryer basket with cooking spray and put lamb chops in a single layer.
4. Air fry for 15 minutes, flipping halfway through cooking time.

calories: 427kcal, carbohydrates: 1g, protein: 31g, fat: 34g, fiber: 1g, sugar: 1g.

STEAK

Serving Size	Prep Time	Cooking time	Total Time
2 Servings	12 Minutes	18 Minutes	30 Minutes

Ingredients

- 2 (170g each) steaks, (2cm thick, rinsed & patted dry)
- 1 tsp. olive oil
- 1/2 tsp. garlic powder
- butter
- Salt & pepper to taste

Directions

1. Preheat the Air Fryer at 400°F/205°C for 5 minutes.
2. Coat steaks with oil. Season both sides with garlic powder, salt & pepper.
3. Spray air fryer basket with cooking spray. Put the steaks in air fryer basket in a single layer.
4. Air Fr for 18 minutes, flipping the steaks halfway through cooking time.
5. When time is up, remove from air fryer, add some butter on top of the steak, cover with foil and allow to rest for 4 minutes. Serve immediately.

calories: 373kcal, protein: 34g, fat: 26g.

BEEF ROAST

Serving Size	Prep Time	Cooking time	Total Time
6 Servings	15 Minutes	45 Minutes	60 Minutes

Ingredients

- 400g beef chuck roast
- 1 tsp. steak seasoning
- 1 package brown gravy mix
- 125ml water
- 4 tbsp. butter
- Parsley or Rosemary to Garnish

Directions

1. Preheat the air fryer at 400°F/205°C for 5 minutes. Season the roast with steak seasoning.
2. Mix the gravy with water and set aside.
3. Carefully spray the basket of the air fryer with cooking spray. Put the roast into the basket and air fry for 15 mins.
4. Once the cooking time is up, remove the roast and place it on sheet pan lined with foil. Roll up the foil around the sides of the roast and put it back to the basket of air fryer. pour the gravy over the roast. Put the butter on top of the roast.
5. Air fry for 40 minutes at 320°F/160°C.
6. Once cooked, let it rest for 5 mins, then slice and serve.

calories: 427kcal, carbohydrates: 1g, protein: 31g, fat: 34g, fiber: 1g, sugar: 1g.

TACO BELL DORITO CRUNCH WRAP

Serving Size	Prep Time	Cooking time	Total Time
6 Servings	24 Minutes	6 Minutes	30 Minutes

Ingredients

- 450g ground beef
- 2 tbsps taco seasoning
- 4-6 burrito size tortillas
- 225g shredded Monterey Jack cheese or Mexican blend cheese
- 1-2 tomatoes sliced
- 1 avocado, diced
- 1 bag Dorito nacho cheese Chips

Directions

1. Brown the ground beef. Add taco seasoning and 120ml water and bring to a boil and cook until water is absorbed.
2. Lay out the tortilla and layer on about 1/2 cup of taco meat, a handful of cheese, tomato slices, Dorito chips, avocado, and a little more cheese. Take the edges of the tortilla and fold it into the middle of taco. Keep folding the sides over each other and into the middle until it is closed.
3. Spray the air fryer basket with cooking spray and place the folded side down in the air fryer basket. Lightly spray the top of the tortilla with cooking spray.
4. Cook at 400°F/205°C for 6 min, or until crunchy. Flip at the halfway point.
5. Serve.

Calories: 539kcal | Carbohydrates: 35g | Protein: 28g | Fat: 32g | Sodium: 798mg | Fiber: 4g | Sugar: 5g

CRESCENT ROLL MEATBALLS

Serving Size	Prep Time	Cooking time	Total Time
4 Servings	10 Minutes	10 Minutes	20 Minutes

Ingredients

- 1 can crescent roll dough
- 120g shredded Mozzarella cheese
- 9-12 Italian style frozen meatballs
- Marinara sauce for dipping

Directions

1. Lay out the crescent roll dough on a flat surface.
2. Place anywhere from 9-12 meatballs on the dough, depends on how big your meatballs are.
3. Cut the dough with a pizza cutter into squares, around the meatballs.
4. Place a layer of cheese on each square of cheese. Completely wrap and cover the meatballs with the dough.
5. Add meatballs in air fryer basket. Cook at 320°F/160°C for 10 minutes.
6. Remove from the air fryer basket and serve with your favorite dipping sauce.

Calories: 367kcal | Carbohydrates: 24g | Protein: 14g | Fat: 25g | Sodium: 683mg | Fiber: 1g | Sugar: 6g

LASAGNA

Serving Size	Prep Time	Cooking time	Total Time
12 Servings	20 Minutes	30 Minutes	50 Minutes

Ingredients

- 340g uncooked penne pasta
- 450g ground beef or ground turkey
- 1 tsp Italian seasoning
- 450g cottage cheese
- 225g cream cheese softened
- 680g jar red pasta sauce
- 170g shredded cheese

Directions

1. Preheat air fryer to 350°F/175°C.
2. Boil the pasta according to instructions on packaging.
3. Brown ground beef. Stir in the Italian seasoning. Set aside.
4. Drain the water from the pasta and return it to the pot. add the cream cheese and cottage cheese and stir until combined.
5. Layer two 8x8 inch/ 20x20 cm pans with half of the pasta mixture, meat, and pasta sauce. Repeat. Add shredded cheese on top. air fry uncovered for 30 minutes.

Calories: 359kcal | Carbohydrates: 27g | Protein: 19g | Fat: 19g | Sodium: 610mg | Fiber: 2g | Sugar: 5g

PIGS IN A BLANKET

Serving Size	Prep Time	Cooking time	Total Time
8 Servings	30 Minutes	6 Minutes	36 Minutes

Ingredients

- 225g cocktail sausages
- 1 sheet puff pastry
- 60g honey mustard
- 1 tbsp black sesame or bagel seasoning
- 1 egg lightly beaten

Directions

1. Defrost the puff pastry enough to unfold it but so it's still firm. Use a sharp knife to cut the puff pastry into 2x4 inch/ 5x10cm pieces.
2. Preheat air fryer to 400°F/205°C.
3. Pat the sausages dry with paper towels. Spoon 1/2 tsp of honey mustard onto the end of each piece of puff pastry, and place a cocktail sausage on top of each.
4. Gently roll the puff pastry around the sausage, pressing to seal together at the end. Brush the top of the puff pastry with egg and sprinkle with bagel seasoning.
5. Set 6-8 pigs in a blanket in air fryer basket, seam side down, with space between each one. Cook for 6 minutes, until crispy. Serve.

Calories: 278kcal | Carbohydrates: 17g | Protein: 6g | Fat: 20g | Sodium: 511mg | Fiber: 1g | Sugar: 2g

CRUSTLESS QUICHE

Serving Size	Prep Time	Cooking time	Total Time
2 Servings	8 Minutes	12 Minutes	20 Minutes

Ingredients

- 4 links sausage remove the casing and cut into pieces
- 2 handfuls spinach
- 1 tbsp water
- 1 small handful of your favorite cheese
- 80ml milk
- 4 eggs beaten
- salt & pepper to taste
- pinch of nutmeg

Directions

1. Cook sausage in the air fryer for 3 minutes at 350°F/ 175°C. Flip, then for 3 minutes at 370°F/185°C.
2. steam the spinach and water in a covered bowl for 2 minutes in the microwave.
3. In a bowl, whisk milk, eggs, salt, pepper, and nutmeg.
4. Place cooked sausage in a sprayed baking dish, top with spinach and cheese. Then add the egg and milk mixture on top
5. Cook at 350°F/175°C for 12 minutes until an inserted toothpick comes out clean.

Calories: 137kcal | Carbohydrates: 4g | Protein: 11g | Fat: 8g | Sodium: 1033mg | Fiber: 1g | Sugar: 2g

BEEF JERKY

Serving Size	Prep Time	Cooking time	Total Time
8 Servings	5 Minutes	60 Minutes	65 Minutes

Ingredients

- 450g flank steak sliced 1/8-inch/0.3cm thick and cut into strips
- 2 tbsp soy sauce
- 1 tbsp worcestershire
- 1 tbsp liquid smoke
- 1 tbsp brown sugar
- 1 tsp salt
- ½ tsp pepper
- ½ tsp meat tenderizer
- ½ tsp garlic powder
- ½ tsp onion powder
- ½ tsp paprika

Directions

1. Whisk soy sauce, worcestershire, liquid smoke, brown sugar, salt, pepper, meat tenderizer, garlic powder, onion powder, and paprika. Add meat to sauce and let marinate for 8 hours.
2. Remove meat from marinade and pat dry with paper towels. Arrange meat in single layers in the air fryer. Air fry at 180°F/82°C for 55 minutes. Cook longer for more tough, chewy jerky.

Calories: 89kcal | Carbohydrates: 3g | Protein: 13g | Fat: 3g | Sodium: 598mg | Fiber: 1g | Sugar: 2g

PEPPERONI STROMBOLI

Serving Size	Prep Time	Cooking time	Total Time
6 Servings	15 Minutes	10 Minutes	25 Minutes

Ingredients

- 220g self rising flour
- 200 g nonfat plain Greek yogurt
- 4 tbsps pizza sauce plus extra for dipping
- 115g shredded mozzarella cheese plus extra for topping
- 75g pepperoni
- 1 egg beaten

Directions

1. In a large mixing bowl, combine flour and Greek yogurt until a thick dough forms. Roll out dough into a 10"x14"/ 25x35cm rectangle on a lightly floured surface. Cut the rectangle in half to form two rectangles.
2. Spread about 2 tbsp pizza sauce on each rectangle, leaving a 2-inch/5cm around the edges. Sprinkle cheese over the sauce on each, then top with pepperoni.
3. Roll the rectangles of dough up into logs. Brush the tops with beaten egg. Sprinkle cheese over top. Use a sharp knife to gently cut diagonal slit, every 2 inches, in the top of each stromboli.
4. Preheat air fryer. Spray air fryer basket with cooking spray. Place stromboli in air fryer basket. Air fry at 340°F/170°C for 10 minutes, until golden brown. Let rest for a few minutes, the cut into slices and serve with extra pizza sauce for dipping.

Calories: 279kcal | Carbohydrates: 29g | Protein: 16g | Fat: 11g | Sodium: 401mg | Fiber: 1g | Sugar: 2g

STUFFED PEPPERS

Serving Size	Prep Time	Cooking time	Total Time
6 Servings	20 Minutes	15 Minutes	65 Minutes

Ingredients

- 6 bell peppers any color
- 450g ground beef
- 2 tbsp taco seasoning
- 160 g cooked rice
- 3 green onions chopped
- 85g black beans
- 165g frozen corn
- cheese to taste

Directions

1. Brown the ground beef. Add the taco. mix.
2. Add the rice, onions, beans, corn and stir.
3. Slice the tops off the peppers and clean out the inside, cut the peppers in half lengthwise, then stuff them with the ground beef mixture.
4. Place up to 6 peppers in the air fryer basket and cook at 350°F/177°C for 10 minutes.
5. Sprinkle cheese on top of the peppers and cook for an additional 5 minutes or until the cheese melts and the peppers are tender.
6. Serve plain or topped with salsa and sour cream.

Calories: 367kcal | Carbohydrates: 25g | Protein: 21g | Fat: 20g | Sodium: 189mg | Fiber: 5g | Sugar: 5g

SWEDISH MEATBALLS

Serving Size	Prep Time	Cooking time	Total Time
4 Servings	20 Minutes	12 Minutes	32 Minutes

Ingredients

- 450g ground beef, lean
- 40g bread crumbs or panko
- 1 tbsp parsley
- 1/4 tsp ground nutmeg
- 1/4 tsp garlic powder
- 1/4 tsp allspice
- 25g diced onions
- salt & pepper to taste
- 1 large egg

Directions

1. in a large mixing bowl, add ground beef, onions, bread crumbs, seasonings, and egg. Mix until combined.
2. Using a cookie scoop roll meatballs, and place them into air fryer basket. Cook at 380°F/195°C for 12 minutes. (shake basket frequently during cooking process)

calories: 580kcal, carbohydrates: 13g, protein: 26g, fat: 47g, fiber: 1g, sugar: 2g.

SPICED BLACK BEAN TACOS

Serving Size	Prep Time	Cooking time	Total Time
4 Servings	5 Minutes	11 Minutes	16 Minutes

Ingredients

- 1 can black beans
- 1 clove garlic, minced
- 1 tbsp taco seasoning
- 1 avocado, diced
- 1 tomato, diced
- 1 bell pepper, diced
- corn tortillas
- any kind of cheese to taste
- 1 lime juice or to taste

Directions

1. Preheat the air fryer 400°F/205°C for 5 minutes.
2. Spray air fryer silicone pot with cooking spray. Add garlic and spray with cooking spray. Roast for 2 minutes.
3. Drain about half of the bean liquid from the can. Add black beans to the silicone pot. Add taco seasoning. Stir. Make sure beans are in a single layer.
4. Air fry at 380°F/193°C for 10 minutes. Stir halfway point.
5. Layer the tortillas with beans, avocados, and tomatoes, feta cheese, and lime juice. serve.

Calories: 170kcal | Carbohydrates: 21g | Protein: 7g | Fat: 8g | Sodium: 56mg | Fiber: 9g | Sugar: 1g

ROASTED FALL VEGETABLES

Serving Size	Prep Time	Cooking time	Total Time
6 Servings	15 Minutes	24 Minutes	40 Minutes

Ingredients

- 1 sweet potato peeled and cubed
- 225g butternut squash peeled and cubed
- 10 baby potatoes sliced in half
- 225g baby bella mushrooms
- 1 red onion cut into wedges
- 1 head of garlic peeled
- 2 tbsp oil
- 2 tbsp balsamic vinegar
- 1 ½ tbsp italian seasoning
- fresh thyme to taste
- Salt & pepper to taste

Directions

1. Preheat the air fryer at 400°F/205°C for 5 minutes.
2. Keep the potatoes, sweet potatoes, and squash separate from the rest of the veggies, but toss everything in the oil and spices.
3. Start with the sweet potatoes, potatoes, and squash in the air fryer basket and cook for 350°F/175°C for 12 minutes.
4. Add remaining veggies and cook for 10-14 more minutes at 350°F/175°C or until tender and crispy.

Calories: 199kcal | Carbohydrates: 36g | Protein: 4g | Fat: 5g | Sodium: 829mg | Fiber: 6g | Sugar: 7g

SQUASH SOUP

Serving Size	Prep Time	Cooking time	Total Time
4 Servings	15 Minutes	30 Minutes	45 Minutes

Ingredients

- 1200g butternut squash, peeled, cut into 2.5cm pieces
- 2 medium carrots, cut into 2.5cm pieces
- 1 large onion, cut into 1 cm-thick wedges
- 2 cloves garlic
- 1 Jalapeno Pepper, seeded
- 4 sprigs fresh thyme
- 2 tbsp. olive oil
- salt

Directions

1. In large bowl, add squash, carrots, onion, whole garlic cloves, Pepper, thyme, 2 tbsp oil and salt. Transfer to air-fryer basket and air fry at 400°F/205°C, stirring halfway through cooking time for 30 minutes.
2. Transfer squash to blender, add 240ml water and puree, gradually adding 720ml water, pureeing until smooth. Reheat if necessary and serve topped with cream and with bread if desired.

280 calories, 15.5 g fat (2.5 g saturated), 5 g protein, 425 mg sodium, 36 g carb, 7 g fiber

POTATO WEDGES

Serving Size	Prep Time	Cooking time	Total Time
4 Servings	5 Minutes	15 Minutes	20 Minutes

Ingredients

- 3-4 large russet potatoes
- 60ml olive oil
- 1 tbsp garlic powder
- 1 tbsp Italian seasoning
- salt or to taste
- ground black pepper to taste
- 50g freshly grated Parmesan

Directions

1. Cut each potato lengthwise in half. Cut each half into three wedges.
2. In a large bowl add potato wedges, oil, garlic powder, Italian seasoning, grated parmesan salt and pepper.
3. Place the potatoes in air fryer basket. Cook at 390°F/200°C for 15 minutes. flip every 5 minutes until crispy and golden brown.
4. Garnish with rosemary and serve with ketchup, ranch, or sauce of choice.

Calories: 402kcal | Carbohydrates: 53g | Protein: 11g | Fat: 17g | Sodium: 206mg | Fiber: 4g | Sugar 2g

FRIED GREEN TOMATOES

Serving Size	Prep Time	Cooking time	Total Time
4 Servings	10 Minutes	10 Minutes	20 Minutes

Ingredients

- 4 large green tomatoes firm
- 2 large eggs
- 60ml milk
- 120g flour
- salt & pepper to taste
- 50g cornmeal
- 50g breadcrumbs
- 2 tbsp grated parmesan
- 1 tbsp Italian seasoning
- olive oil spray

Directions

1. In a small bowl add eggs and whisk. Add milk. stir.
2. In another bowl add flour, salt, and pepper.
3. In bowl add cornmeal, bread crumbs, and parmesan cheese.
4. Dredge each tomato slice in eggs, then in flour, and lastly the cornmeal mix. Add tomatoes to air fryer basket and spray tops with cooking spray.
5. Cook at 400°F/205°C for 6 minutes, then flip and spray with cooking spray and cook for more 5 minutes.

PLANTAINS

Serving Size	Prep Time	Cooking time	Total Time
4 Servings	2 Minutes	15 Minutes	17 Minutes

Ingredients

- 2 Medium yellow plantains
- 2 tsp oil
- salt to taste
- ⅛ tsp cayenne pepper

Directions

1. Wash and dry plantains, Peel the skin out, then cut diagonally.
2. Transfer cut plantains into a bowl, add oil, salt, and pepper, toss to combine.
3. Arrange plantains in air fryer basket and air fry at 350°F/180°C for 17 mins flipping half way through cooking time.
4. Serve with your favorite side dish or sauce.

Calories: 18kcal | Carbohydrates: 1g | Protein: 1g | Fat: 2g | Sodium: 37mg | Fiber: 1g | Sugar 1g

KALE CHIPS

Serving Size	Prep Time	Cooking time	Total Time
2 Servings	10 Minutes	4 Minutes	14 Minutes

Ingredients

- ½ bunch Kale (about 8 Stalks)
- Cooking spray
- ⅛ tsp salt
- ½ tsp ranch powder

Directions

1. Remove the middle stalk from each leaf, cut leaves into medium sizes & wash
2. Drain leaves & transfer to a paper towel lined tray.
3. Spray with cooking spray, Toss to coat the leave, sprinkle with salt and ranch seasoning, toss to coat.
4. Spread on the air fryer basket in single layer. Put an air fryer rack over it to prevent leaves flying around while it bakes.
5. Bake at 380°F / 194°C for 4-5 mins. Shake the basket half way through.

Calories: 87kcal | Carbohydrates: 11g | Protein: 3g | Fat: 3g | Sodium: 152mg | Fiber: 1g

FALAFEL

Serving Size	Prep Time	Cooking time	Total Time
4 Servings	2 Minutes	15 Minutes	17 Minutes

Ingredients

- 200g dried chickpeas, soaked overnight
- 40g parsley
- 30g chopped onion
- 2 medium cloves garlic
- 1 tbsp olive oil
- 1 tbsp lemon juice
- 1 tbsp ground cumin
- ½ tsp salt
- ¼ tsp baking soda
- 1 to 3 tbsp water, if needed

Directions

1. Drain chickpeas and transfer to a food processor. Add parsley, onion, garlic, oil, lemon juice, cumin, salt and baking soda; process, adding water as needed, until finely ground and the mixture just holds together. Using about 3 tbsps per patty, shape into twelve patties.
2. coat air fryer basket with cooking spray. Place the patties in a single layer in the basket and coat the tops with cooking spray. (you may have to cook in batches.)
3. Cook the patties at 375°F / 190°C for 12 minutes, flipping them over halfway through and coating the tops with cooking spray.

Calories: 216kcal | Carbohydrates: 13g | Protein: 6g | Fat: 6g | Sodium: 37mg | Fiber: 383g | Sugar 5g

AIR FRYER APPLES

Serving Size	Prep Time	Cooking time	Total Time
4 Servings	5 Minutes	15 Minutes	17 Minutes

Ingredients

- 6 apples
- 1 tsp vegetable oil
- 1 tbsp maple syrup
- 2 tsp sugar
- 1/2 tsp cinnamon

Directions

1. Peel, core and slice the apples. Toss them in vegetable oil.
2. Place the apples in a single layer in the air fryer basket.
3. Air fry the apples at 400°F/205°C for 14 minutes.
4. Place the apples in a bowl and stir in the maple syrup, sugar and cinnamon.

EGGPLANT

Serving Size	Prep Time	Cooking time	Total Time
4 Servings	5 Minutes	10 Minutes	15 Minutes

Ingredients

- 1 Large Eggplant
- 1 tsp Paprika
- ½ tsp Garlic
- ¼ tsp Oregano
- ¼ tsp Black Pepper
- 1 tbsp Olive oil

Directions

1. Preheat the air fryer to 360°F/180°C
2. cut eggplant into fries, cubes, or wedges. Add into a bowl, then add in the paprika, garlic, oregano, pepper, salt, and oil. Mix.
3. Arrange the eggplant in the air fryer basket in a single layer.
4. Air fry for 10 minutes. stirring halfway through cooking time.

Calories: 61kcal | Carbohydrates: 7g | Protein: 1g | Fat: 4g | Sodium: 293mg | Fiber: 4g | Sugar 4g

CAJUN SCALLOPS

Serving Size	Prep Time	Cooking time	Total Time
2 Servings	5 Minutes	6 Minutes	11 Minutes

Ingredients

- 4-6 Sea scallops
- Cooking spray
- salt to taste
- Cajun seasoning

Directions

1. Preheat air fryer 400°F/205°C.
2. rinse scallops in cold water. Remove the side muscle with your fingers and pat dry with paper towels.
3. line air fryer basket with aluminium foil and spray with cooking spray.
4. spray the scallops with cooking spray and season with salt and coat with cajun seasoning .
5. Place all the scallops in the air fryer and cook for 3 minutes. Flip and cook for 3 more minutes.
6. Serve with pasta, salad or alongside roasted vegetables.

ROASTED OKRA

Serving Size	Prep Time	Cooking time	Total Time
2 Servings	5 Minutes	10 Minutes	15 Minutes

Ingredients

- 500g Fresh or Frozen Okra
- 1 Tsp Garlic Salt
- Cooking Spray

Directions

1. Coat the air fryer basket with cooking spray.
2. Add okra to the basket and coat with cooking spray and garlic salt.
3. Air Fry at 355°F/180°C for 10 minutes, stir halfway through cooking time.

Calories: 99kcal | Carbohydrates: 8g | Protein: 3g | Fat: 7g | Sodium: 802mg | Fiber: 4g | Sugar 4g

GREEN BEANS

Serving Size	Prep Time	Cooking time	Total Time
2 Servings	2 Minutes	10 Minutes	12 Minutes

Ingredients

- 360g frozen green beans
- 1 tbsp soy sauce
- 1 tbsp butter
- 2 tsp light brown sugar

Directions

1. Add green beans into air fryer basket. Shake around until evenly distributed.
2. Air fry at 350°F / 176°C for 10 minutes.
3. in a microwave-safe dish, add soy sauce, butter and brown sugar. Microwave on high for one minute. stir.
4. Transfer tgreen beans to a bowl. Toss with soy sauce glaze. Serve.

RATATOUILLE GNOCCHI

Serving Size	Prep Time	Cooking time	Total Time
4 Servings	10 Minutes	15 Minutes	25 Minutes

Ingredients

- 450g gnocchi
- 4 cloves garlic minced
- 4 cups mixed vegetables zucchini, eggplants, tomatoes, bell pepper, red onion, all cut into bite sized pieces
- 50g olive oil
- 2 tbsp balsamic vinegar
- salt & pepper to taste
- 1 tbsp oil

Directions

1. In a large bowl, mix vegetables with olive oil, garlic, balsamic vinegar, salt, and pepper.
2. In a separate bowl, mix the gnocchi together with 1 tbsp oil. Season with salt and pepper.
3. Place the vegetables in the air fryer basket then add the gnocchi on top. Cook at 400°F/205°C for 15 minutes. stir at the halfway point.
4. Remove from the air fryer basket and serve.

Calories: 436kcal | Carbohydrates: 68g | Protein: 6g | Fat: 17g | Sodium: 401mg | Fiber: 9g | Sugar: 9g

SMASHED POTATOES

Serving Size	Prep Time	Cooking time	Total Time
4 Servings	5 Minutes	30 Minutes	35 Minutes

Ingredients

- 450g baby yellow potatoes
- Olive oil spray
- salt & pepper to taste
- 2 tbsp butter, melted
- 2 cloves garlic, minced
- 30g grated Parmesan cheese

Directions

1. Add potatoes to air fryer and spray with oil spray. season with salt and pepper.
2. Cook the potatoes at 400°F/205°C for 15 minutes.
3. Remove the potatoes from the air fryer and smash them with a rolling pin.
4. Add potatoes back to the air fryer basket. (cook them in two batches).
5. In a small bowl, stir melted butter and garlic.
6. Bush the potatoes with garlic butter and cook for an additional 10 minutes until golden brown.
7. Sprinkle with parmesan and serve.

Calories: 225kcal | Carbohydrates: 26g | Protein: 5g | Fat: 12g | Sodium: 240mg | Fiber: 3g | Sugar: 1g

AIR FRYER PINEAPPLE

Serving Size	Prep Time	Cooking time	Total Time
4 Servings	5 Minutes	15 Minutes	20 Minutes

Ingredients

- 1 whole pineapple peeled and cored
- 30g light brown sugar
- 1 tsp cinnamon

Directions

1. Preheat air fryer to 375°F/190°C.
2. Slice pineapple into 8 slices. Set aside.
3. In a small bowl, mix together brown sugar and cinnamon. Spinkle mixture over the pineapple rings.
4. Place pineapple in the air fryer basket and airfry for 8 minutes each side.
5. Serve warm.

Calories: 45kcal | Carbohydrates: 14g | Protein: 1g | Fat: 1g | Sodium: 4mg | Fiber: 1g | Sugar: 13g

GARLIC MUSHROOMS

Serving Size	Prep Time	Cooking time	Total Time
2 Servings	8 Minutes	12 Minutes	20 Minutes

Ingredients

- 225g mushrooms, (halved)
- 2 tbsp. olive oil
- 1/2 tsp. garlic powder
- 1 tsp. Worcestershire/soy sauce
- Juice of 1 lemon
- 1 tbsp. parsley, (chopped)
- Salt & pepper to taste

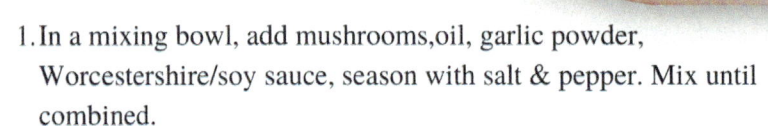

Directions

1. In a mixing bowl, add mushrooms, oil, garlic powder, Worcestershire/soy sauce, season with salt & pepper. Mix until combined.
2. Air fry at 380°F/195°C for 12 minutes, stirring half way through cooking time.
3. When time is up, remove from air fryer, put lemon juice and parsley. Serve warm.

calories: 92kcal, carbohydrates: 4g, protein: 3g, fat: 7g, fiber: 1g, sugar: 2g.

ROASTED POTATOES

Serving Size	Prep Time	Cooking time	Total Time
4 Servings	5 Minutes	15 Minutes	20 Minutes

Ingredients

- 700g small potatoes, (halved)
- 1/2 tsp garlic powder
- Salt & pepper to taste
- Cooking spray

Directions

1. Preheat air fryer to 400°F/205°C with basket inside.
2. In a large mixing bowl, mix together all ingredients.
3. Spray air fryer basket with cooking spray.
4. In batches, air fry at 400°F/205°C for 15 mins, flipping halfway through cooking time.
5. Serve.

133kcal, Fat: 1g, Carbohydrates: 30g, Protein: 4g

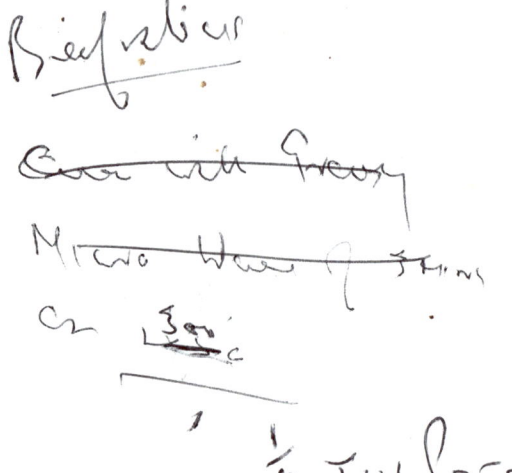

BUTTERNUT SQUASH

Serving Size	Prep Time	Cooking time	Total Time
4 Servings	5 Minutes	25 Minutes	30 Minutes

Ingredients

- 1 small butternut squash, (peeled & cut into 1.5cm cubes)
- 2 tbsp oil
- 1/2 tsp paprika
- 1/2 tsp garlic powder
- Salt & pepper to taste

Directions

1. In a large mixing bowl, add oil, paprika, garlic powder, season with salt & pepper. Mix until combined. Add butternut squash cubes and mix to coat with seasoning.
2. Add the squash to air fryer basket in a single layer (cook in batches).
3. Air Fry at 380°F/195°C for 24 minutes. Flipping halfway through cooking time.
4. Serve warm.

calories: 128kcal, carbohydrates: 17g, protein: 2g, fat: 7g, fiber: 3g, sugar: 3g.

ROASTED BRUSSELS SPROUTS

Serving Size	Prep Time	Cooking time	Total Time
4 Servings	5 Minutes	20 Minutes	25 Minutes

Ingredients

- 500g brussels sprouts , (cut into bite-sized pieces)
- 3 tbsp oil
- 1 tbsp balsamic vinegar
- Salt & pepper to taste

Directions

1. In a large mixing bowl, add brussels sprouts, oil and balsamic vinegar, season with salt & pepper. Toss the brussels sprouts to fully coat with the seasoning.
2. Add the brussels sprouts to the air fryer basket.
3. Air fry at 360°F/180°C for about 20 minutes. Flipping halfway through cooking time.
4. Season with salt & pepper if needed. Serve

calories: 83kcal, carbohydrates: 10g, protein: 3g, fat: 3g, fiber: 4g, sugar: 3g

ACORN SQUASH

Serving Size	Prep Time	Cooking time	Total Time
4 Servings	15 Minutes	20 Minutes	35 Minutes

Ingredients

- 1 acorn squash
- 4 tbsp melted butter
- 2 tbsp brown sugar
- 1/2 tsp salt

Toppings:

- melted butter
- chopped roasted nuts

Directions

1. Cut the squash in half from top to bottom. Scoop seeds out. Cut the squash into half rings, 1.5-cm thick.
2. In a small mixing bowl, add melted butter, brown sugar, and salt. Toss the acorn squash in the butter mixture until coated.
3. Put acorn squash rings in the air fryer basket.
4. Air Fry at 375°F/190°C for 20 minutes until tender, flipping halfway through cooking time
5. Serve with melted butter, chopped nuts.

calories: calories: 126kcal, carbohydrates: 13g, protein: 1g, fat: 9g, fiber: 2g, sugar: 2g.

ASPARAGUS

Serving Size	Prep Time	Cooking time	Total Time
5 Servings	5 Minutes	10 Minutes	15 Minutes

Ingredients

- 500g fresh asparagus, ends trimmed
- 2 tsp oil
- Salt & pepper to taste

Directions

1. Coat asparagus with oil and season with salt & pepper.
2. Air Fry at 375°F/190°C for 10 minutes, flipping halfway through cooking time.
3. Remove from air fryer. Serve.

calories: 32kcal, carbohydrates: 4g, protein: 2g, fat: 1g, fiber: 2g, sugar: 2g

GARLIC CARROTS

Serving Size	Prep Time	Cooking time	Total Time
2 Servings	5 Minutes	15 Minutes	20 Minutes

Ingredients

- 250g carrots, (peeled & cut lengthways)
- 2 tsp oil
- 2 garlic cloves, (minced)
- 1/2 tsp dried thyme
- 1/2 tsp dried basil
- Salt & pepper to taste

Directions

1. In a large mixing bowl, add oil, all seasoning. mix until combined. Add the carrots and toss to evenly coat with seasoning.
2. Put carrots in the air fryer basket.
3. Air fry at 360°F/180°C for 15 minutes.

calories: 83kcal, carbohydrates: 11g, protein: 1g, fat: 4g, fiber: 3g, sugar: 5g.

SWEET POTATO FRIES

Serving Size	Prep Time	Cooking time	Total Time
4 Servings	8 Minutes	22 Minutes	31 Minutes

Ingredients

- 450g sweet potatoes, (peeled & cut into 0.5cm fries)
- 2 tsp oil
- 1/4 tsp garlic powder
- Salt & pepper to taste

Directions

1. In a large mixing bowl, add sweet potatoes, and all seasoning. Toss to evenly coat all the fries with oil and seasonings.
2. Put the sweet potatoes in the air fryer basket in a single layer.
3. Air Fry at 375°F/190°C for about 22 minutes, Flipping then couple of times through cooking time.

calories: 116kcal, carbohydrates: 23g, protein: 2g, fat: 2g, fiber: 3g, sugar: 5g.

CORN ON THE COB

Serving Size	Prep Time	Cooking time	Total Time
2 Servings	5 Minutes	17 Minutes	22 Minutes

Ingredients

- 2 fresh ears of corn, (cleaned)
- 2 tbsp butter
- Cooking spray
- Salt & pepper to taste

Directions

1. Spray all sides of the corn with cooking spray. Season with salt & pepper.
2. Air Fry at 365°F/185°C for 17 minutes, flipping halfway through cooking time.
3. Spread butter on the corn and adjust seasoning if desired. Serve.

calories: 177kcal, carbohydrates: 16g, protein: 3g, fat: 12g, fiber: 1g, sugar: 5g.

GREEN BEAN CASSEROLE

Serving Size	Prep Time	Cooking time	Total Time
6 Servings	5 Minutes	15 Minutes	20 Minutes

Ingredients

- 400g green beans, (fresh or frozen)
- 1 can condensed cream of mushroom soup
- 180g fried onions, (divided)
- Salt & pepper to taste

Directions

1. Preheat the Air fryer to 350°F/175°C. Grease a 15cm square cooking pan.
2. In a large mixing bowl, add beans, mushroom soup, and half of the fried onion. Mix until all combined.
3. Pour into the prepared pan.
4. Put in the air fryer.
5. Air fry for 15 minutes.
6. Remove from the air fryer and Serve topped with remaining fried onion.

Calories: 230kcal, Carbohydrates: 19g, Protein: 4g, Fat: 15g, Fiber: 1g, Sugar: 2g.

CAULIFLOWER WITH GARLIC

Serving Size	Prep Time	Cooking time	Total Time
4 Servings	5 Minutes	18 Minutes	25 Minutes

Ingredients

- 1 small head cauliflower (cut into bite-size pieces)
- 2 tbsp oil
- 1/2 tsp garlic powder
- 1/2 tsp smoked paprika
- 1/2 tsp chilli flakes
- Salt & pepper to taste
- Parsley , for garnish

Directions

1. In a large mixing bowl, add cauliflower florets, oil, all the seasoning. Mix until all florets coated with seasoning.
2. Put the cauliflower into air fryer basket in a single layer.
3. Air Fry at 360°F/180°C for 18 minutes, flipping halfway through cooking time.
4. Remove from air fryer, garnish with chopped parsley.

calories: 98kcal, carbohydrates: 8g, protein: 3g, fat: 7g, fiber: 3g, sugar: 3g

ROASTED PARMESAN TOMATOES

Serving Size	Prep Time	Cooking time	Total Time
2 Servings	5 Minutes	3 Minutes	8 Minutes

Ingredients

- 1-2 tomatoes
- salt and pepper to taste
- grated parmesan cheese to taste
- mozzarella cheese to taste
- fresh basil leaves to taste
- olive oil

Directions

1. Slice the tomatoes into thick slices and place into a greased air fryer basket.
2. Top the tomatoes with salt, pepper, grated parmesan cheese, and mozzarella cheese.
3. Cook at 400°F/200°C for 3 minutes.
4. Top with fresh basil and enjoy.

Calories: 159kcal | Carbohydrates: 7g | Protein: 11g | Fat: 10g | Sodium: 400mg | Fiber: 1g | Sugar: 4g

CRISPY ONION

Serving Size	Prep Time	Cooking time	Total Time
2 Servings	5 Minutes	25 Minutes	30 Minutes

Ingredients

- 2 medium to large yellow onions
- 1 tbsp cooking oil

Directions

1. Peel and cut onion into thin slices.
2. Drizzle oil over the slices and separate the rings.
3. Place the onion rings in the air fryer basket. Cook at 300°F/150°C for 10 min. Gently mix the rings halfway through cooking time.
4. lower the temperature down to 240°F/115°C and continue cooking for 18 minutes. After every 5 min gently mix the rings.

Calories: 568kcal | Carbohydrates: 35g | Protein: 25g | Fat: 37g | Sodium: 1157mg | Fiber: 1g | Sugar: 12g

VEGETARIAN QUESADILLA

Serving Size	Prep Time	Cooking time	Total Time
4 Servings	10 Minutes	5 Minutes	15 Minutes

Ingredients

- 8 medium flour tortillas
- 100g shredded Colby jack cheese
- 1 red bell pepper, chopped
- ½ onion, chopped
- 1 can black beans, rinsed & drained
- 1 can corn, rinsed & drained

Directions

1. Sauté the veggies. Place the veggies in the air fryer basket. Spray with oil. Sauté in the air fryer at 380°F/193°C for 5 minutes.
2. Layer each tortilla with cheese, veggies, and black beans. Fold in half.
3. Secure. Place in the air fryer basket and keep the quesadillas secure by using toothpicks.
4. Air fry for 370°F/187°C for 5 minutes, or until crispy and melty.

Calories: 402kcal | Carbohydrates: 47g | Protein: 18g | Fat: 16g | Sodium: 642mg | Fiber: 8g | Sugar: 3g

MOZZARELLA STICKS

Serving Size	Prep Time	Freezing Time	Total Time
4 Servings	10 Minutes	2H 30M	3H 10M

Ingredients

- 6 mozzarella cheese sticks
- 2 tbsp all-purpose flour
- Salt & pepper to taste
- 2 eggs divided
- 20g panko breadcrumbs
- ½ tsp Italian seasoning
- ¼ tsp garlic powder
- Cooking spray

Directions

1. Cut each of the mozzarella stick in half. Freeze the sticks for at least an hour in a Ziploc safe bag.
2. Set up three small bowls for breading mozzarella sticks
3. In the first bowl, mix together the flour, salt, and pepper. In the second bowl, beat 1 egg. In a third bowl, mix panko, Italian seasoning, and garlic powder.
4. Coat each mozzarella stick in flour mixture, egg, and then panko. (Keep the leftover panko mixture.)
5. Place the mozzarella sticks on a baking sheet and freeze mozzarella sticks for 1 hour.
6. In a small bowl, beat the second egg. remove mozzarella sticks out of freezer and dip them in egg, then coat them in panko mixture again.
7. Freeze the mozzarella sticks for another 30 minutes.
8. Spray air fryer basket and place mozzarella sticks. spray with oil and cook at 400°F/200°C for 7-10 minutes.

Calories: 185kcal | Carbohydrates: 8g | Protein: 13g | Fat: 11g | Sodium: 471mg | Fiber: 1g | Sugar: 1g

GINGERBREAD BITES

Serving Size	Prep Time	Cooking time	Total Time
9 Servings	10 Minutes	9 Minutes	19 Minutes

Ingredients

- 1 can crescent roll dough
- 225g cream cheese
- 1 tbsp plus 100g sugar divided
- ½ tbsp ground allspice
- ¾ tbsp ground cinnamon
- ½ tbsp ground ginger
- ¾ tsp ground cloves
- ¾ tsp ground nutmeg

Directions

1. Mix together all the spices & 100g sugar in a medium bowl. Set aside.
2. add remaining sugar and cream cheese in a small bowl. Use a fork to mix.
3. Unroll the crescent dough. Evenly place a tbsp of the cream cheese mixture every couple inches from each other on on the crescent dough.
4. with a pizza cutter cut the dough evenly into squares around the cream cheese.
5. Gently fold crescent dough to cover cream cheese.
6. Dip and cover the bites with the spice mixture.
7. Place bites into a lightly sprayed air fryer basket on parchment paper for 8 to 9 minutes at 350°F/175°C.
8. Remove from the air fryer basket and enjoy.

Calories: 203kcal | Carbohydrates: 22g | Protein: 2g | Fat: 13g | Sodium: 251mg | Fiber: 1g | Sugar: 14g

PASTA CHIPS

Serving Size	Prep Time	Cooking time	Total Time
4 Servings	15 Minutes	12 Minutes	27 Minutes

Ingredients

- 225g dried pasta
- 1 tbsp. olive oil
- 1 tsp. garlic powder
- 40g Parmesan cheese
- 1 tsp. Italian seasoning
- Salt & pepper to taste

Directions

1. Cook pasta according to package directions until tender.
2. Once pasta cooked, drain and transfer into a large mixing bowl. Add oil, garlic powder, Parmesan, and season with salt, pepper & Italian seasoning. Mix until pasta coated.
3. Air fry in a single layer at 380°F/195°C for 8 mins, stirring every 3 mins. Cook until golden and crispy.
4. Serve with sauce of choice.

Calories: 380kcal, Carbohydrates: 47g, Protein: 26g, Fat: 27g, Fiber: 2g, Sugar: 8g

EGG ROLLS

Serving Size	Prep Time	Cooking time	Total Time
12 Servings	20 Minutes	12 Minutes	32 Minutes

Ingredients

- 2 tbsp vegetable oil
- 1/2 tsp minced garlic
- 1/2 tsp minced ginger
- handful finely chopped celery
- 180g coleslaw mix
- 225g ground chicken
- 3 tbsp oyster sauce
- 1 tbsp soy sauce
- 1 tsp sesame oil
- 1 tbsp sriracha
- 1 chopped green onion
- 12 egg roll wrappers

Directions

1. Heat oil in a pan and saute fry garlic, ginger, celery till fragrant. Add the coleslaw mix and cook till the cabbage is wilted.
2. Add the ground chicken, oyster sauce, soy sauce, sesame oil and sriracha. cook for 4 minutes. Once chicken is cooked and there is no liquid, stir in the green onions and remove from heat.
3. place the egg roll wrapper. Place a tbsp of filling in the bottom half and wrap corner over the filling. turn both sides over the wrapper and then continue rolling like a burrito. Seal the edges with water or a beaten egg.
4. Spray air fryer basket with cooking spray. Place the egg rolls in the basket and spray the tops of egg rolls with cooking spray. Cook at 400°F/200°C for 6 minutes. Then flip the egg rolls and cook for an additional 6 minutes.

Calories: 79kcal | Carbohydrates: 9g | Protein: 5g | Fat: 4g | Sodium: 327mg | Fiber: 1g | Sugar: 14g

TOASTED RAVIOLI

Serving Size	Prep Time	Cooking time	Total Time
4 Servings	10 Minutes	10 Minutes	20 Minutes

Ingredients

- 2 large eggs
- 80g Italian seasoned breadcrumbs
- 45g grated parmesan cheese
- 420g package cheese ravioli
- cooking spray
- marinara sauce for serving

Directions

1. In a small bowl add eggs and whisk. In another bowl add breadcrumbs and parmesan cheese. mix.
2. Dip each ravioli into the egg mixture and then into the breadcrumb mixture.
3. Continue with each ravioli and place into air fryer basket.
4. Cook at 360°F/180°C for 4 minutes. Spray with cooking spray and flip and cook for 4 minutes until golden.

Calories: 148kcal, Carbohydrates: 11g, Protein: 10g, Fat: 7g, Fiber: 1g, Sugar: 1g.

CHEESE WONTONS

Serving Size	Prep Time	Cooking time	Total Time
4 Servings	10 Minutes	10 Minutes	20 Minutes

Ingredients

- 240g cream cheese softened
- 2 tbsp green onion, chopped
- 1/2 tsp garlic powder
- 1/4 tsp salt
- wonton wrappers
- cooking spray

Directions

1. In a small bowl add the cream cheese, green onions, garlic powder and salt and whisk until creamy.
2. Lay a wonton wrapper on a non stick surface. wet the edges of the wonton wrapper. Add about a tsp of the cream cheese filling and bring up each corner creating a star and seal tightly.
3. Spray the basket of an air fryer with olive oil spray. Add the wontons to the basket and lightly spray with olive oil. Cook at 370°F/190°C for 8 minutes.

Calories: 195kcal | Carbohydrates: 3g | Protein: 3g | Fat: 19g | Sodium: 328mg | Fiber: 1g | Sugar: 2g

CHIN CHIN

Serving Size	Prep Time	Cooking time	Total Time
10 Servings	15 Minutes	15 Minutes	30 Minutes

Ingredients

- 280 g all purpose flour
- 90 g granulated sugar
- 120g salted butter melted
- ½ tsp baking powder
- ½ tsp ground nutmeg
- 1 large egg
- 60ml milk

Directions

1. in a bowl, Mix sugar flour and nutmeg. Add the melted butter, milk and beaten egg into dry mixture
2. Mix to form a dough Let dough rest for about 5 minutes
3. On a floured surface, roll out dough with a rolling pin, cut into strips first horizontally then vertically with pizza wheel.
4. Divide dough into 2 batches.
5. Arrange first batch in the basket of the air fryer and air fry at 350°F/180°C for 15-18 minutes
6. Repeat for the other batches

Calories: 234kcal, Carbohydrates: 38g, Protein: 5g, Fat: 7g, Fiber: 1g, Sugar: 11g.

JALAPEÑO POPPERS

Serving Size	Prep Time	Cooking time	Total Time
12 Servings	10 Minutes	5 Minutes	15 Minutes

Ingredients

- 12 jalapeño peppers sliced in halves, deseeded
- 180g cream cheese softened
- 1 tsp garlic powder
- 120g cheddar, shredded
- 3 tbsp Panko bread crumbs
- 1 tbsp butter melted

Directions

1. Preheat the Air Fryer to 390°F/200°C.
2. In a medium bowl, add cream cheese, garlic powder and cheddar. mix.
3. In a small bowl, combine panko crumbs with melted butter.
4. Take each jalapeño half, and fill with cream cheese mixture then top with panko breadcrumbs.
5. Place in the Air Fryer basket, and air fry for 6 minutes.

Calories: 110kcal | Carbohydrates: 4g | Protein: 4g | Fat: 19g | Sodium: 113mg | Fiber: 1g | Sugar: 1g

STUFFED PEPPERS

Serving Size	Prep Time	Cooking time	Total Time
4 Servings	10 Minutes	15 Minutes	25 Minutes

Ingredients

- 4-6 Bell Peppers destemed and seeds removed
- 400g diced tomatoes
- 400g tomato sauce
- 200g cooked rice
- 1 can black beans drained and rinsed
- 1-2 tsp Italian Seasoning
- 50g mozzarella cheese
- 1 tbsp parmesan cheese

Directions

1. Combine diced tomatoes, tomato sauce, rice, beans and seasoning together.
2. Place mixture into scooped out bell peppers. Fill bell peppers to top with mixture.
3. Place stuffed peppers into air fryer basket. Cook at 360°F/180°C. for 12 minutes. Remove from air fryer but keep in basket.
4. Top stuffed peppers with cheese mixture and cook for another 3 minutes.

Calories: 156kcal, Carbohydrates: 23g, Protein: 6g, Fat: 4g, Fiber: 4g, Sugar: 7g.

TORTILLA CHIPS

Serving Size	Prep Time	Cooking time	Total Time
2 Servings	10 Minutes	5 Minutes	15 Minutes

Ingredients

- 12 corn tortillas
- 1 tbsp olive oil
- 2 tsp salt
- 2 tbsp Italian spices
- guacamole, for serving

Directions

1. Preheat the air fryer to 350°F/180°C.
2. brush the tortillas with olive oil on both sides.
3. Sprinkle the tortillas with the salt and Italian spices on both sides.
4. Cut each tortilla into 6 wedges.
5. Working in batches, add the tortilla wedges to the air fryer in a single layer air fry for 5 minutes until golden brown and crispy.
6. Serve with guacamole.

FRIED RICE

Serving Size	Prep Time	Cooking time	Total Time
4 Servings	10 Minutes	15 Minutes	25 Minutes

Ingredients

- 550g rice cooked and cold
- 180g frozen vegetables (carrots, corn, broccoli, and peas or edamame)
- 50ml soy sauce
- 1 tbsp oil
- 2 eggs scrambled.

Directions

1. into a large mixing bowl, add rice. Add frozen vegetables. add eggs. add soy sauce and oil . Mix until combined.
2. Transfer rice mixture to an oven-safe container.
3. Place container into air fryer basket. Cook for 15 minutes at 360°F/182°C. Stir three times during cook time.
4. Serve warm.

Calories: 589kcal, Carbohydrates: 115g, Protein: 13g, Fat: 7g, Fiber: 2g, Sugar: 1g.

SAUSAGE CRESCENT CHEESE BALLS

Serving Size	Prep Time	Cooking time	Total Time
12 Servings	10 Minutes	8 Minutes	18 Minutes

Ingredients

- 450g breakfast sausage
- 240g sharp cheddar cheese, shredded
- 240g can refrigerated crescent rolls
- 2 tbsp all-purpose flour,

Directions

1. in a large bowl, Mix sausage and cheese.
2. Unroll dough on a parchment paper. Dust each side of dough with a tbsp of flour.
3. Use a pizza cutter to cut dough into (1/4-inch/1/2-cm) pieces.
4. add the crescent pieces into the sausage mixture. mix it until evenly mixed in.
5. Shape into 1 1/4-inch balls.
6. Line air fryer basket with parchment paper.
7. Arrange 8 balls in basket. There should be plenty of space around them.
8. Refrigerate remaining sausage balls.
9. Air fry for 12 minutes at 400°F/200°C, flipping them over after 6 minutes.
10. Repeat with remaining sausage balls.

Calories: 262kcal, Carbohydrates: 9g, Protein: 11g, Fat: 20g, Fiber: 1g, Sugar: 2g.

ONION RINGS

Serving Size	Prep Time	Cooking time	Total Time
6 Servings	12 Minutes	12 Minutes	24 Minutes

Ingredients

- 60g all-purpose flour
- 1 tsp paprika
- 1 tsp salt, divided
- 120ml buttermilk
- 1 egg
- 70g Panko crumbs
- 2 tbsp olive oil
- 1 large yellow, sliced and separated into rings
- Cooking spray

Directions

1. in a bowl, add flour, paprika, and 1/2 tsp of salt. mix
2. In a second bowl, whisk together buttermilk and egg. Whisk in 1/4 cup of the flour mixture.
3. In a third bowl, combine Panko crumbs, 1/2 tsp salt, and 2 tbsp oil. Stir.
4. Dredge onion rings in flour mixture, then dip in buttermilk mixture and dredge in Panko crumb mixture.
5. Place in Air Fryer basket. Cook (working in batches) at 400°F/200°C for 13 minutes. Turn them over halfway through and spray with cooking spray.

Calories: 152kcal, Carbohydrates: 18g, Protein: g, Fat: 3g, Fiber: 1g, Sugar: 2g. Sodium 493mg .

EGGPLANT PARMESAN

Serving Size	Prep Time	Cooking time	Total Time
4 Servings	15 Minutes	25 Minutes	45 Minutes

Ingredients

- 1 large eggplan
- 60g bread crumbs
- 3 tbsp grated parmesan cheese
- salt to taste
- 1 tsp Italian seasoning
- 3 tbsp flour
- 1 egg + 1 tbsp water
- Cooking spray
- 220g marinara sauce
- 60g grated mozzarella cheese

Directions

1. Cut eggplant into roughly ½"/1.5cm slices. Rub salt on both sides of slices and leave it for 15 mins.
2. in a small bowl, mix egg with water and flour to prepare the batter.
3. In a medium plate combine bread crumbs, parmesan cheese, Italian seasoning, and salt. Mix.
4. Dip each eggplant slice in patter evenly. Dip battered slices in breadcrumb mix to coat.
5. Place breaded eggplant slices on a dry plate and spray with cooking.
6. Preheat the Air Fryer to 360°F/182°C. Put the eggplant slices on basket and cook for 8 min.
7. Top the slices with marinara sauce and spread mozzarella cheese on it. Cook the eggplant for another 2 mins.
8. Serve warm.

JICAMA FRIES

Serving Size	Prep Time	Cooking time	Total Time
6 Servings	12 Minutes	28 Minutes	40 Minutes

Ingredients

- 900g jicama (peeled and cut into fries)
- 2 tbsp Olive oil
- 1/2 tsp Garlic powder
- 1 tsp Cumin
- 1 tsp salt
- 1/4 tsp Black pepper

Directions

1. Boil a large pot of water on the stove. Add tfries and boil for 18 to 25 minutes, until no longer crunchy. Time will vary depending on the thickness of your fries.
2. When the jicama is not crunchy anymore, remove and pat dry.
3.
4. Set the air fryer to 400°F/205°C and let it preheat for 3 minutes.
5. Place the fries into a large bowl. Drizzle with oil and season with garlic powder, cumin, and salt. Toss to coat.
6. Working in batches t, arrange jicama in the air fryer basket in a single layer. Air fry for12 minutes, until golden. Repeat with remaining fries.

alories: 109kcal, carbohydrates: 16g, protein: 2g, fat: 5g, fiber: 9g, sugar: 3g

FETTA NUGGETS

Serving Size	Prep Time	Cooking time	Total Time
18 Servings	10 Minutes	10 Minutes	20 Minutes

Ingredients

- 4 tbsp flour
- 1 tsp onion powder
- 1/2 tsp. pepper
- 1 tsp dried chilli flakes
- 1 egg
- 30g panko breadcrumbs
- 40g sesame seeds
- 180g Fetta Cheese, (cut into 2cm cubes)
- Salt & pepper to taste
- Barbecue sauce
- 75g barbecue sauce
- 1 1/2 tsp apple cider vinegar
- 1/2 tsp dried chilli flakes

Directions

1. In a large mixing bowl, add flour, onion powder, chilli flakes, and season with salt & pepper. In another bowl, add eggs and whisk them. In a third bowl, add breadcrumbs and sesame seeds.
2. Toss fetta cheese cubes in the flour mixture, then dip in egg, then coat breadcrumb mixture (you may need to work in batches).
3. Preheat air fryer to 360°F/180°C. Plut fetta cubes, in a single layer, in the air fryer basket. Cook for 6 minutes until golden.
4. Mix all Barbecue sauce ingredients in a bowl.
5. When time is up, remove fetta cubes from air fryer. Serve fetta with sauce.

calories: 50kcal, carbohydrates: 5g, protein: 8g, fat: 6g, sugar: 1.5g.

CRISPY TOFU BITES

Serving Size	Prep Time	Cooking time	Total Time
6 Servings	5 Minutes	35 Minutes	40 Minutes

Ingredients

- 400g firm/extra firm tofu , (drained)
- 1/2 tsp. lemon zest
- 1/2 tsp. garlic powder
- Salt & pepper to taste
- Cooking spray

Directions

1. Preheat air fryer at 400°F/205°C for 5 minutes. Spray air fryer basket with cooking spray.
2. Squeeze the excess water from the tofu block. Cut tofu into 2cm thick slices.
3. In a large mixing bowl, add tofu cubes and coat evenly with cooking spray. Sprinkle half the amount of spices. Stir to coat.
4. Put tofu in air fryer basket in a single layer, (you may need to work in batches).
5. Air fry for 30 minutes until golden brown, flipping half way through cooking time.
6. When the time is up, remove from air fryer. Allow to cool and serve.

calories: 96kcal, carbohydrates: 4g, protein: 10g, fat: 4g, fiber: 1g, sugar: 1g

JOJO POTATO WEDGES

Serving Size	Prep Time	Cooking time	Total Time
6 Servings	10 Minutes	20 Minutes	30 Minutes

Ingredients

- 4 large russet potatoes, (scrubbed, cut into wedges & soaked in cold water for 30 mins)
- 100g flour
- 1 tsp. garlic powder
- 1 tsp. onion powder
- 1 tsp. smoked paprika
- Pinch of cayenne
- 2 large egg
- 2 tbsp. water
- Salt & pepper to taste
- Cooking spray

Directions

1. In a large mixing bowl, add flour, garlic powder, onion powder, paprika, cayenne and season with salt & pepper. Mix until combined.
2. In a medium mixing bowl, whisk eggs and water.
3. Pat the potato dry, then dredge them in the flour mixture, then dredge them into the egg then back into the flour.
4. Put wedges in the air fryer basket in a single layer. Spray the wedges with cooking spray.
5. Air fry at 400°F/205°C for 18 minutes flipping & spraying them with cooking spray halfway through cooking time.
6. When time is up, remove from air fryer, and serve with favorite dipping sauce.

calories: 290kcal, carbohydrates: 50g, protein: 8g, fat: 4g, fiber: 5g, sugar: 2g

FRIED PICKLES

Serving Size	Prep Time	Cooking time	Total Time
10 Servings	10 Minutes	10 Minutes	20 Minutes

Ingredients

- 3 whole Pickled cucumber, (sliced into 1.5cm slices)
- 30g plain flour

For the batter

- 1 large egg
- 1 tbsp mustard
- 125ml water
- 90g plain flour

For the coating

- 120g breadcrumbs
- ½ tsp garlic powder
- ½ tsp onion powder
- ½ tsp cumin
- ½ tsp smoked paprika
- Salt & pepper to taste

Directions

1. Preheat air fryer at 420°F/215°C for 10 minutes.
2. In a large mixing bowl, add flour. In another bowl, add egg, mustard and water, whisk them. Sift in the flour a few tbsp at a time, until a thick batter is formed. In a third bowl, add breadcrumbs and all the seasonings.
3. Dip each pickle slice into the flour, then wet batter and then into the breadcrumbs.
4. Spray the air fryer basket with cooking spray. Put pickle slices in the air fryer basket and spread them into an even layer. Spray pickles with cooking spray.
5. Air Fry for about 8 minutes, until golden.
6. Serve with your favorite dip.

calories: 115kcal, carbohydrates: 18g, protein: 4g, fat: 3g, fiber: 1g, sugar: 1g.

SPINACH DIP

Serving Size	Prep Time	Cooking time	Total Time
8 Servings	7 Minutes	38 Minutes	45 Minutes

Ingredients

- 230g cream cheese, (softened)
- 160g frozen spinach, (thawed & drained)
- 100g grated Parmesan cheese
- 225g mayonnaise
- 75g tinned white turnips, (drained)
- 1 onion, (minced)
- 1/4 tsp. garlic powder
- 1 tsp. black pepper
- Cooking spray

Directions

1. In a large mixing bowl, mix all ingredients together until combined. Mix to completely combine. Transfer the mixture into baking dish coated with cooking spray.
2. Air Fry at 300°F/150°C for 30 minutes, stirring the dip half way through cooking time.
3. When time is up, Stir again. Increase heat to 340°F/170°C and then air fry for 8 minutes until golden brown.

calories: 356kcal, carbohydrates: 4g, protein: 7g, fat: 34g, fiber: 1g, sugar: 2g,

CHEESY MUSHROOM

Serving Size	Prep Time	Cooking time	Total Time
10 Servings	10 Minutes	10 Minutes	20 Minutes

Ingredients

- 230g button mushrooms
- 120g softened cream cheese
- 1/2 tsp garlic powder
- 1/4 tsp paprika
- 1/4 tsp chili powder
- 50g grated cheese
- Salt & pepper to taste

Directions

1. Remove mushroom stems, then dice the stems and set aside half of the diced stems.
2. In a large mixing bowl, add cream cheese, garlic powder, paprika, chili powder, season with salt & pepper. Mix until smooth. Add in the reserved diced mushroom stems.
3. Spray the mushroom tops with cooking spray. Fill the mushroom with the cream cheese mixture.
4. Put mushrooms in the air fryer basket in a single layer (cook in batches).
5. Air fry at 360°F/180°C for 8 minutes.
6. Top with grated cheese, air fry for another 2 minutes until the cheese is melted.
7. Serve warm or at room temperature.

calories: 55kcal, carbohydrates: 1g, protein: 2g, fat: 5g, fiber: 1g, sugar: 1g.

SWEET POTATO ROLLS

Serving Size	Prep Time	Cooking time	Total Time
5 Servings	5 Minutes	15 Minutes	20 Minutes

Ingredients

- 250g ml) cooked & mashed sweet potato
- 250g self rising flour
- Cooking spray

Directions

1. In a large mixing bowl, add sweet potato and flour. Mix until a dough ball forms.
2. Knead dough ball until smooth, on a floured surface. Don't over-knead it.
3. Divide the dough into 6 equal pieces. Roll to form 6 balls. Let rest for 30 minutes.
4. Spray air fryer basket with cooking spray. Put dough balls in the basket. Spray the top with cooking spray.
5. Air Fry at 320°F/165°C for 14 minutes.
6. Remove from air fryer, allow to cool and sprinkle with salt or sugar and serve.

calories: 117kcal, carbohydrates: 25g, protein: 3g, fat: 1g, fiber: 2g, sugar: 3g.

GARLIC BREAD

Serving Size	Prep Time	Cooking time	Total Time
4 Servings	4 Minutes	6 Minutes	10 Minutes

Ingredients

- ½ loaf French Bread
- 4 tbsp butter, (softened)
- 4 garlic cloves, (minced)
- 4 tsp chopped parsley

Directions

1. Cut bread into evenly sized slices.
2. In a small mixing bowl, add butter, garlic, and parsley. Mix until combined.
3. Spread butter mixture on each slice of bread.
4. Put bread slices in the air fryer basket.
5. Air fry at 370°F/185°C for 6 minutes until golden & crispy.

Calories: 161kcal, Carbohydrates: 31g, Protein: 7g, Fat: 1g, Fiber: 1g, Sugar: 2g.

CRISPY BREADED BROCCOLI BITES

Serving Size	Prep Time	Cooking time	Total Time
2 Servings	7 Minutes	15 Minutes	22 Minutes

Ingredients

- 250g fresh broccoli, (cut into bite-sized pieces)
- 1/2 tsp garlic powder
- 1 egg
- 50g bread crumbs
- 2 tbsp grated Parmesan cheese
- Salt & pepper to taste
- Cooking spray

Directions

1. Preheat air fryer at 350°F / 180°C.
2. In a large mixing bowl, add broccoli florets, all the seasonings, egg and mix to coat the broccoli.
3. In another mixing bowl, add breadcrumbs and Parmesan cheese.
4. Dip broccoli in the breadcrumb mixture. Spray the breaded broccoli with cooking spray until fully coated.
5. Spray air fryer basket with cooking spray. Put broccoli in a single layer in the basket.
6. Air Fry for 15 minutes. Flipping and spraying with cooking spray halfway through cooking time.
7. Serve with your favorite dip.

alories: 147kcal, carbohydrates: 18g, protein: 10g, fat: 5g, fiber: 4g, sugar: 3g

TURNIPS

Serving Size	Prep Time	Cooking time	Total Time
4 Servings	10 Minutes	15 Minutes	30 Minutes

Ingredients

- 3 medium turnips peeled and cut into fries
- 2 tbsp olive oil
- ½ tsp garlic powder
- ½ tsp onion powder
- ½ tsp paprika
- salt, pepper, and red chili flakes to taste

Directions

1. Preheat the air fryer to 400°F/205°C
2. Add the turnips to a mixing bowl. Drizzle with oil.
3. Sprinkle the seasonings over the turnips.Toss to combine .
4. Place the turnips on air fryer basket.
5. Air fry for 15 minutes, shaking halfway through.

Calories: 90kcal, Carbohydrates: 6g, Protein: 1g, Fat: 7g, Fiber: g, Sugar: 4g.

ARANCINI

Serving Size	Prep Time	Cooking time	Total Time
12 Servings	10 Minutes	10 Minutes	20 Minutes

Ingredients

- 400g cooked arborio rice, room temperature
- 200g mozzarella cheese, shredded
- 2 tbsp fresh parsley, chopped
- 75g Italian breadcrumbs
- 20g grated parmesan cheese
- 2 tbsp all-purpose flour
- 1 tbsp Italian seasoning
- 1 tsp sea salt
- 2 large eggs, beaten

Directions

1. Mix arborio rice with shredded mozzarella and parsley.
2. Roll into 14 balls (If it is too sticky put it in fridge for 30 minutes). preheat air fryer to 360°F/182°C.
3. In a small bowl mix breadcrumbs, flour, Italian seasoning, and salt. set aside.
4. dip a rice ball into beaten egg and then roll into breading mixture covering all sides.
5. Put rice balls in air fryer and cook for 16 minutes, flipping them halfway with tongs. work in batches if needed.
6. Serve with marinara sauce and lightly garnished with fresh parsley

calories: 128kcal, carbohydrates: 14g, protein: 6g, fat: 5g, fiber: 1g, sugar: 11g

COURGETTE FRIES

Serving Size	Prep Time	Cooking time	Total Time
6 Servings	10 Minutes	8 Minutes	18 Minutes

Ingredients

- 2 medium courgette, (cut into fries)
- 180g plain flour
- 2 eggs, (beaten)
- 250g breadcrumbs
- 60g grated Parmesan cheese
- Salt & pepper to taste

Directions

1. In a medium mixing bowl, add flour. In another mixing bowl, add beaten eggs. In a 3rd bowl, mix breadcrumbs, cheese and season with salt & pepper.
2. Dip each courgette fries in the flour, shake off the excess. Then coat with eggs. Finally coat it with breadcrumb mixture.
3. Put it in air fryer basket. Coat them again with cooking spray. (you may need to work in batches)
4. Air fry at 400°F/205°C for 8 mins until browned.

Per Serving: 230kcal
Fat: 5g, Carbohydrates:20g, Protein:10g

CROUTONS

Serving Size | **Prep Time** | **Cooking time** | **Total Time**
10 Servings | **5 Minutes** | **7 Minutes** | **12 Minutes**

Ingredients

- 4 slices bread cut into small cubes
- 4 tbsp melted butter
- ½ tsp onion powder
- ½ tsp garlic powder
- ¼ tsp salt

Directions

1. In a large mixing bowl, add bread cubes.
2. Toss bread cubes with butter until each cube is coated.
3. Add the onion powder, garlic powder, salt, and parsley. Mix to coat bread cubes with the seasonings.
4. Add the bread cubes to the air fryer basket.
5. Air Fry at 395°F/200°C for 7 minutes, tossing halfway through the cooking time.

Calories: 81kcal, Carbohydrates: 6g, Protein: 1g, Fat: 6g, Fiber: 1g, Sugar: 1g

MARGHERITA PIZZA

Serving Size	Prep Time	Cooking time	Total Time
1 Servings	5 Minutes	8 Minutes	13 Minutes

Ingredients

- 1 thin crust pre-made cooked pizza crust
- 3 tbsp pizza sauce
- 1 tomato thinly sliced
- 5 slices of fresh mozzarella
- fresh basil
- 1 tsp olive oil

Directions

1. Spread the pizza sauce over the prepared pizza crust. Place the tomato slices evenly apart on the crust. Add mozzarella in between the tomato slices.
2. Place in the basket of the air fryer and cook at 350°F/177°C for 8 minutes until cheese is melted.
3. Serve immediately.

Calories: 1573kcal | Carbohydrates: 202g | Protein: 69g | Fat: 54g | Sodium: 323mg | Fiber: 8g | Sugar: 13g

EGGPLANT PIZZA

Serving Size	Prep Time	Cooking time	Total Time
4 Servings	5 Minutes	10 Minutes	15 Minutes

Ingredients

- 1 medium sized eggplant sliced into ½ inch/1.5cm slices
- 120nl marinara sauce.
- 120g Cheddar or mozzarella cheese
- 70g Pepperoni or favorite toppings
- 1 tbsp Italian seasoning

Directions

1. Pat eggplant with a paper towel to remove excess moisture. Place eggplant in a single layer in the air fryer and cook at 400°F/200°C for 2 minutes. Then flip and cook for 2 minute.
2. Spread sauce evenly over eggplant. Top with cheese and pepperoni and sprinkle with Italian seasoning.
3. Cook for 5 minutes until lightly brown on the top

calories: 239kcal, carbohydrates: 10g, protein: 13g, fat: 17g, fiber: 4g, sugar: 6g.

BREAKFAST PIZZAS WITH ENGLISH MUFFINS

Serving Size	Prep Time	Cooking time	Total Time
6 Servings	5 Minutes	5 Minutes	10 Minutes

Ingredients

- 6 Eggs Cooked & Scrambled
- 450g Ground Sausage Cooked
- 50g Shredded Colby Jack Cheese
- marinara sauce (optional)
- 3 English Muffins Sliced in Half (6 Halves)
- Olive Oil Spray
- Fennel Seed Optional

Directions

1. Spray air fryer basket with cooking spray.
2. Place 3 English Muffins halves in the air fryer.
3. Spray English muffins with cooking spray and top with cooked eggs and cooked sausage. Add cheese to the top of each one.
4. Cook at 355°F/180°C for 5 minutes.
5. Carefully remove and repeat for the remaining muffins.
6. Serve.

Calories: 429kcal | Carbohydrates: 15g | Protein: 20g | Fat: 32g | Sodium: 885mg | Fiber: 1g | Sugar: 1g

ZUCCHINI PIZZA BITES

Serving Size	Prep Time	Cooking time	Total Time
3 Servings	8 Minutes	10 Minutes	18 Minutes

Ingredients

- 2 zucchini (medium sized)
- 180ml Marinara Sauce
- 120g shredded mozzarella cheese
- 150g pepperoni
- 1 tbsp olive oil (for spraying)

Directions

1. Slice the zucchini into slices that are about ¼ inch/0.5cm thick.
2. Lay the zucchini slices flat in the air fryer basket. Do not overcrowd. You will need to do this in batches. Spray the slices with cooking spray and cook at 400°F/200°C for 4 minutes.
3. Add marinara sauce, shredded mozzarella cheese and pepperoni on top of each zucchini slice. Place the basket back into air fryer and cook for 6 minutes until cheese melts.
4. Repeat with remaining batches. let cool on a wire cooling rack.

PIZZA BOMBS

Serving Size	Prep Time	Cooking time	Total Time
16 BOMBS	15 Minutes	5 Minutes	20 Minutes

Ingredients

- 1 can (8 count) refrigerated biscuits
- 32 pieces pepperoni
- 225g mozzarella cheese, cut into 16 cubes
- 60g melted butter
- ½ tsp garlic powder
- ½ tsp Italian seasoning

Directions

1. Separate each biscuit in half to form 16 biscuit pieces.
2. Cut the pepperoni slices into quarters and place 8 quarters of pepperoni in the center of each biscuit. Place one mozzarella cube in the center of each biscuit.
3. Fold up the edges of the biscuit to fold the pepperoni and cheese into the center. Roll into a ball, sealing the edges.
4. Place the biscuits in air fryer basket in even layer, leaving space between each.
5. In a small bowl add the butter, garlic powder, and Italian seasoning, and whisk to combine. Brush the butter mixture over the dough.
6. Air fry at 350°F / 180°C. for 6 minutes until golden brown and cooked through.

Calories: 168kcal | Carbohydrates: 16g | Protein: 6g | Fat: 9g | Sodium: 476mg | Fiber: 1g | Sugar: 2g

PIZZA POCKETS

Serving Size	Prep Time	Cooking time	Total Time
8 Servings	10 Minutes	10 Minutes	10 Minutes

Ingredients

- 1 can refrigerated biscuits (8-count)
- 60ml marinara sauce
- 100g shredded mozzarella cheese
- pizza toppings of choice
- 1 large egg, whisked with 1 tbsp water
- 60g grated Parmesan cheese

Directions

1. Separate the biscuits into 8 rounds and then divide each biscuit in half to form 16 rounds.
2. Arrange 8 rounds. Add 2 tsp marinara sauce, 1 tbsp shredded mozzarella cheese and any additional pizza toppings into the center of each round.
3. Place a second round on top of fillings, pressing around the edges. Using a fork, seal edges of pizza pockets. Brush with egg wash then sprinkle with grated Parmesan cheese.
4. Arrange pizza pockets in air fryer basket. cook at 300°F/150°C for 10 minutes until golden brown.
5. Remove from air fryer, let them cool slightly then serve.

PIZZA ROLLS

Serving Size	Prep Time	Cooking time	Total Time
4 Servings	10 Minutes	6 Minutes	16 Minutes

Ingredients

- 1 can pizza sheet
- Pizza sauce
- 100g shredded mozzarella cheese
- 100g shredded cheddar cheese
- ½ ham sliced
- Italian seasoning to taste
- garlic powder to taste
- salt and pepper to taste

Directions

1. Unroll the pizza dough onto a lightly floured surface. Brush pizza sauce over the entire sheet. Sprinkle with Italian seasoning, garlic powder, and salt and pepper.
2. Sprinkle mozzarella cheese and cheddar over . Spread the ham on top of the cheese in a single layer. Add your favorite additional pizza toppings. press down on the toppings.
3. Tightly roll the pizza dough lengthwise until it is a long roll, like a cinnamon roll. With a knife, cut the log into 8 pieces.
4. Cook at 350°F/175°C for 8 minutes until the crust is golden.

Calories: 291kcal | Carbohydrates: 47g | Protein: 11g | Fat: 7g | Sodium: 836mg | Fiber: 1g | Sugar: 6g

PEPPERONI PIZZA EGG ROLLS

Serving Size	Prep Time	Cooking time	Total Time
2 Servings	15 Minutes	15 Minutes	30 Minutes

Ingredients

- 120g pepperoni slices, (chopped)
- 120g shredded mozzarella cheese
- 120ml marinara sauce
- 1 tsp Italian seasoning
- 1 bell pepper, (chopped)
- 15 egg roll or spring roll wrappers
- Cooking spray

Directions

1. In a medium bowl, add pepperoni, mozzarella, marinara, Italian seasonings and bell peppers. Mix until combined.
2. Add 2 tbsp of filling to each egg roll wrapper. Tuck and roll wrapper around filling. Brush corner of the wrapper with water to seal the end.
3. Spray rolls with cooking spray. Put rolls in the air fryer basket in a single layer (cook in batches).
4. Air Fry 383°F/195°C for 15 minutes, flipping halfway through cooking time.
5. Remove from air fryer. Allow to cool a little, and serve with your favorite sauce.

calories: 109kcal, carbohydrates: 9g, protein: 5g, fat: 6g, fiber: 1g, sugar: 1g.

BISCUIT MINI PIZZAS

Serving Size	Prep Time	Cooking time	Total Time
8 Servings	5 Minutes	5 Minutes	10 Minutes

Ingredients

- 1 can regular refrigerated biscuits
- 60ml pizza sauce

Desired Toppings
- mini pepperonis
- sliced olives
- 120g shredded mozzarella cheese
- olive oil spray

Directions

1. Lightly spray air fryer basket with cooking spray. Flatten each biscuit in the bottom of air fryer basket. Spread with 1 tbsp pizza sauce.
2. Add desired toppings. (mini pepperonis and olives).
3. Sprinkle with Parmesan Cheese.
4. Air fry at 350°F/175°C for 5 minutes or until golden.

Calories: 255kcal | Carbohydrates: 29g | Protein: 7g | Fat: 13g | Sodium: 672mg | Fiber: 1g | Sugar: 6g

PIZOOKIE

Serving Size	Prep Time	Cooking time	Total Time
8 Servings	15 Minutes	10 Minutes	25 Minutes

Ingredients

- 125g all purpose white flour
- ¼ tsp salt
- ¼ tsp baking soda
- 6 tbsp unsalted butter melted and slightly cooled
- 110g light brown sugar
- 50 g granulated sugar
- 1 egg
- 1 tsp vanilla
- 180g chocolate chips

Directions

1. Preheat the air fryer at 400°F/200°C for 5 minutes.
2. In a bowl, whisk the flour, salt, and baking soda.
3. In another bowl, whisk melted butter and sugars until combined. Then, add egg and vanilla and mix.
4. Using a spatula, fold dry ingredients into the wet ingredients until just combined; do not over mix. add chocolate chips and spread cookie dough into a pan that will fit in your air fryer.
5. Cook at 320°F/160°C for 7 minutes, then let the pan sit inside the warm air fryer for a couple of minutes to let it finish setting.

Calories: 266kcal | Carbohydrates: 39g | Protein: 2g | Fat: 12g | Sodium: 124mg | Fiber: 1g | Sugar: 26g

PEANUT BUTTER AND JELLY

Serving Size	Prep Time	Cooking time	Total Time
2 Servings	5 Minutes	6 Minutes	11 Minutes

Ingredients

- 4 slices bread
- 2 tbsp butter softened
- 2 tbsp jelly
- 2 tbsp peanut butter or almond butter

Directions

1. Spread peanut butter on one side of a slice of bread, spread jelly on one side of another slice.
2. Cover the bread to make a closed sandwich.
3. Next spread some butter on the outside of the sandwich.
4. Then place the sandwich buttered side down in the air fryer basket, spread some more butter on the unbuttered side.
5. Air fry at 400°F/204°C for 4 minutes. Then flip . And air fry for another 3 minutes until golden brown.
6. Serve and enjoy.

Calories: 405kcal | Carbohydrates: 44g | Protein: 10g | Fat: 22g | Sodium: 430mg | Fiber: 3g | Sugar: 15g

106

AIR FRYER BISCUITS

Serving Size	Prep Time	Cooking time	Total Time
8 Servings	15 Minutes	10 Minutes	25 Minutes

Ingredients

- 240g all-purpose flour
- 3 tsps baking powder
- 1/2 tsp salt
- 7 tbsp cold butter cut into little squares
- 240g cold milk
- 2 tbsp melted butter to brush on the tops

Directions

1. In a large bowl, Mix flour, baking powder and salt. Cut in the cold butter until the mixture resembles gravel. Add milk and stir to form a dough. Do not over mix.
2. With a spoon, scoop out 10 biscuits.
3. Place biscuits, spaced apart, in air fryer basket. You may need to cook in 2 batches.
4. Cook at 400°F/205°C for 8 minutes, then open the basket and brush on the melted butter. Continue cooking until lightly golden brown on top, for 2 more minutes.

Calories: 197kcal | Carbohydrates: 12g | Protein: 3g | Fat: 11g | Sodium: 344mg | Fiber: 1g | Sugar: 1g

BLUEBERRY MUFFIN

Serving Size	Prep Time	Cooking time	Total Time
3 MUFFIN	5 Minutes	10 Minutes	15 Minutes

Ingredients

- 1 egg
- 65g sugar
- 80 ml oil
- 2 tbsp water
- ¼ tsp vanilla extract
- 1 tsp lemon zest
- 80g flour
- ½ tsp baking powder
- Pinch of salt
- 75g blueberries

Directions

1. In a bowl, Mix the wet ingredients and the zest. Set aside.
2. In a smaller bowl whisk the dry ingredients. Add the dry ingredients to the wet ingredients.
3. Spray 3 silicon muffin liners with cooking spray and set aside. Scoop batter into papers with an ice cream scoop.
4. Air fry at 350°F/180°C. for 17 minutes

Calories: 39kcal | Carbohydrates: 15g | Protein: 2g | Fat: 3g | fiber 11g. Sugar: 0g

CANNOLI

Serving Size	Prep Time	Cooking time	Total Time
8 Servings	15 Minutes	15 Minutes	30 Minutes

Ingredients

- 750g ricotta cheese
- 100g powdered sugar
- 1 tbsp orange zest
- ½ tsp salt
- 200g dark brown sugar
- 420g refrigerated piecrusts
- 1 large egg white, beaten
- 120g mini chocolate chips
- 30g coarsely chopped roasted pistachios

Directions

1. Place ricotta in a strainer lined with cheesecloth, and press until excess liquid drips out. Place strained ricotta in a medium bowl, and stir in powdered sugar, orange zest, and salt. Spoon into a piping bag. Chill. Place dark brown sugar on a plate. Set aside.
2. Roll out piecrusts on a lightly floured surface to 1/16-inch/1mm thickness. Cut out 16 (3 1/2-inch/7cm) circles. Wrap circles around cannoli molds, brushing edge with egg white to seal. Lightly brush entire wrapper with egg white. Roll in brown sugar to coat.
3. Add a few at a time to coated with cooking spray air fryer basket. Cook at 400°F/205°C for 7 minutes until golden. Carefully and cool 1 minute before twisting cannoli mold out of shell. Let cool completely. Repeat with remaining shells.
4. Place chocolate chips and pistachios in separate small bowls. Pipe ricotta mixture into each cooled cannoli shell. Dip 1 end in either chocolate chips or pistachios. Dust with powdered sugar. Serve immediately.

BANANA MUFFINS

Serving Size	Prep Time	Cooking time	Total Time
7 Servings	10 Minutes	14 Minutes	24 Minutes

Ingredients

- 3 very ripe bananas
- 2 large eggs (beaten)
- 120g salted butter (melted)
- 75g monk-fruit sweetener/ or regular sugar
- 1 tsp vanilla extract
- 1 tsp baking soda
- ¼ tsp baking powder
- 220g All purpose flour

Directions

1. Spray silicon muffin liners with cooking spray and set aside
2. Mash Bananas in a bowl, add Sweetener, butter, eggs, vanilla and mix to combine. Add flour, baking powder and baking soda to the wet ingredients, then mix to combine.
3. Scoop batter into prepared muffin liners and Air fry at 330°F/166°C for 14 mins until tooth pick comes out clean

Calories: 170 kcal | Carbohydrates: 15g | Protein: 2g | Fat: 7g | Sodium: 80mg | Fiber: 1g | Sugar: 4g

CHOCOLATE BANANA MUFFINS

Serving Size	Prep Time	Cooking time	Total Time
9 Servings	10 Minutes	14 Minutes	24 Minutes

Ingredients

- 3 medium Very ripe bananas
- 2 large eggs
- 120g salted butter (melted)
- 200g sugar
- 1 tsp vanilla extract
- 1 tsp baking soda
- ¼ tsp baking powder
- 120g All purpose flour
- 60g cocoa powder
- 70g cup chocolate chips

Directions

1. Spray silicon muffin liners with cooking spray and set aside
2. in a bowl, mash bananas, add melted butter, eggs, vanilla and mix to combine.
3. Add cocoa powder, flour, baking powder and baking soda and mix. Add chocolate chips.
4. Scoop batter into prepared muffin liners. Transfer to air fryer basket
5. Air fry at 330°F / 165°C for 14 mins until tooth pick comes out clean.

Calories: 210 kcal | Carbohydrates: 25g | Protein: 3g | Fat: 7g | Sodium: 236mg | Fiber: 7g | Sugar: 13g

SHORTBREAD COOKIES

Serving Size	Prep Time	Cooking time	Total Time
8 Servings	10 Minutes	8 Minutes	18 Minutes

Ingredients

- 6 tbsp Butter
- 50g powdered sugar
- 100g all purpose flour

Directions

1. Whip butter and sugar till light and fluffy. Add flour and mix to combine. The dough would be crumbly, do not over mix. Use your hands to bring the dough together to form a ball.
2. Roll dough into a log. Wrap tightly in cling film and refrigerate for 30 mins.
3. Remove the dough from the fridge, unwrap and slice into ½ inch/1.5cm round discs
4. Line air fryer basket with parchment paper making sure there is at least 2 inches/5cm of room round to ensure proper heat and air circulation.
5. Transfer cookies to air fryer basket and bake at 330°F/166°C for 10 mins. Let cookies cool for 5 mins in the air fryer before transferring to a cooling rack with a cookie lifter to cool completely.

Calories: 51 kcal | Carbohydrates: 8g | Protein: 1g | Fat: 5g | Sodium: 37mg | Fiber: 1g | Sugar: 3g

SCOTCH PANCAKES

Serving Size	Prep Time	Cooking time	Total Time
10 Servings	15 Minutes	8 Minutes	25 Minutes

Ingredients

- 200g wheat flour
- 1 tbsp. baking powder
- 1 tbsp. granulated sugar
- 1 tsp. ground cinnamon
- 1 large egg
- 300ml milk
- Pinch of salt

Directions

1. In a large mixing bowl, add flour, baking powder, sugar, cinnamon and salt. Add the egg and milk and whisk with a whisk.
2. Set pancake batter aside for a few minutes, turn air fryer to 400°F/205°C.
3. Spray 4 pie tins with cooking spray. Put 1/4 cup of batter into each pie tin. Spread batter evenly.
4. Air fry 8 minutes until pancakes are golden brown.
5. Remove pancakes from air fryer. Allow to cool slightly, then remove with a spatula. Serve.

Calories: 121kcal | Carbohydrates: 19g | Protein: 4g | Fat: 3g | Saturated Fat: 1g | fiber 1g.

LEMONADE SCONES

Serving Size	Prep Time	Cooking time	Total Time
16 Servings	45 Minutes	15 Minutes	60 Minutes

Ingredients

- 500g self-raising flour
- 70g caster sugar
- 300ml heavy cream
- 180ml lemonade
- 1 tsp vanilla extract
- Milk, for brushing

Directions

1. In a large mixing bowl, add flour, sugar, cream, lemonade and vanilla. Gently mix until dough just comes together.
2. Transfer dough onto a floured surface. Knead until just smooth. Press the dough to a 2.5cm thick round. Cut out 5.5cm scones. Repeat to make 16 scones.
3. Spray air fryer basket with cooking. Place 5 scones in basket. Brush top with milk. (cook in batches)
4. Air fry at 320°F/160°C for 15 minutes.
5. Serve warm.

Calories: 405kcal | Carbohydrates: 44g | Protein: 10g | Fat: 22g | Sodium: 430mg | Fiber: 3g | Sugar: 15g

APPLE HAND PIES

Serving Size	Prep Time	Cooking time	Total Time
8 Servings	5 Minutes	10 Minutes	15 Minutes

Ingredients

Apple Hand Pies

- 420g refrigerated pie crusts or homemade - two crusts
- 600g apple pie filling Homemade or store bought

Glaze

- 50g powdered sugar
- 1/8 tsp milk or water

Directions

1. Cut out 8 circles in the prepared pie crust.
2. Top 4 pie crust circles with apple pie filling and top with additional pie crust.
3. Use a fork to crimp pie edges together and a knife to slice an "=" in the center.
4. Place the pies in the basket of the air fryer and cook at 350°F/180°C for 10 minutes or until the crust begins to turn golden brown.
5. Meanwhile, prepare the glaze by stirring together the confectioners sugar and milk/water.
6. Drizzle the glaze over finished pies and serve.

Calories: 209kcal | Carbohydrates: 24g | Protein: 3g | Fat: 11g | fiber 11g. Sugar: 4g

PEANUT BUTTER COOKIES

Serving Size	Prep Time	Cooking time	Total Time
9 Servings	10 Minutes	7 Minutes	17 Minutes

Ingredients

- 220g all purpose flour
- ¾ tsp baking soda
- ½ tsp salt
- 120g butter room temperature
- 125g peanut butter smooth
- 110 g brown sugar
- 100 g sugar
- 2 egg
- 2 tbsp milk

Directions

1. In a medium bowl, mix purpose flour and baking soda. Set aside.
2. In another bowl, mix butter and peanut butter Add sugars and mix until combined. add the egg and milk. Mix to combine. Slowly add flour mixture in small increments. Mix until just combined. Do not overmix.
3. Roll a tbsp of cookie dough into a ball. Use a fork to flatten the cookie. Place cookies into air fryer basket.
4. Air fry at 350°F/180°C for 7 minutes a.
5. Remove cookies from air fryer. Cookies should rest until completely cool to strengthen.

Calories: 355kcal | Carbohydrates: 44g | Protein: 6g | Fat: 18g | Sodium: 382mg | Fiber: 2g | Sugar: 25g

BLUEBERRY HAND PIES

Serving Size	Prep Time	Cooking time	Total Time
8 Servings	15 Minutes	12 Minutes	27 Minutes

Ingredients

- 125g blueberries
- 2.5 tbsp caster sugar
- 1 tsp lemon juice
- 1 pinch salt
- 320g refrigerated pie crust or shortcrust pastry roll
- water
- vanilla sugar to sprinkle on top

Directions

1. in a medium bowl, mix blueberries, sugar, lemon juice, and salt.
2. Roll out the piecrusts and cut out 6-8 (4-inch/10cm) individual circles.
3. Place 1 tbsp of blueberry filling in center of each circle. Moisten edges of dough with water, and fold the dough over the filling to form a half moon shape. Using a fork, gently crimp the edges of the piecrust together.
4. Spray hand pies with cooking spray and sprinkle with vanilla sugar.
5. Preheat the air fryer to 350°F/180°C. Place 3-4 hand pies in single layer inside air fryer basket.
6. Cook for 12 mins until golden brown.
7. Let the pies cool for at least 10 mins before serving.

Calories: 251kcal | Carbohydrates: 30g | Protein: 3g | Fat: 11g | fiber 1g. Sugar: 5g

JELLY DONUTS

Serving Size	Prep Time	Cooking time	Total Time
4 Servings	10 Minutes	5 Minutes	15 Minutes

Ingredients

- 1 can (8 count) refrigerated biscuits
- 120g seedless raspberry jelly
- 1 tbsp butter, melted
- 100g powdered sugar

Directions

1. Preheat air fryer to 320°F/165°C.
2. Place biscuits inside the air fryer in a single layer and cook for 6 minutes until golden brown.
3. Remove biscuits from air fryer and set aside.
4. Place sugar into a wide bowl with a flat bottom.
5. Baste butter on all sides of the donut and roll in the sugar to cover completely. Complete with all remaining donuts.
6. Using a long cake tip, pipe 1-2 tbsp of raspberry jelly into each donut.

Calories: 252kcal | Carbohydrates: 45g | Protein: 3g | Fat: 17g | Sodium: 502mg | Fiber: 0g | Sugar: 23g

CARAMELIZED BANANAS

Serving Size	Prep Time	Cooking time	Total Time
4 Servings	1 Minutes	6 Minutes	7 Minutes

Ingredients

- 2 bananas
- 1/4 lemon, juiced
- 1 tbsp coconut sugar
- 1 tbsp cinnamon
- optional toppings: nuts, coconut cream, yogurt, granola.

Directions

1. Peel and slice bananas straight down the middle, length wise
2. Squeeze lemon juice over top of each banana
3. mix cinnamon with coconut sugar, then sprinkle over top of the bananas until coated
4. Place into parchment lined air fryer basket, cook at for 8 minutes at 400°F/205°C
5. Once removed of the air fryer, eat as is or on top of oatmeal or pancakes.

BUTTERMILK DROP BISCUITS

Serving Size	Prep Time	Cooking time	Total Time
10 Servings	12 Minutes	8 Minutes	20 Minutes

Ingredients

- 360g all-purpose flour
- 1 tbsp sugar
- 2 1/2 tsps baking powder
- 1/2 tsp salt
- 6 tbsp cold butter, cubed
- 280g cold buttermilk
- cooking spray
- melted butter, optional

Directions

1. in a large bowl. Whisk flour, sugar, baking powder, and salt. Add the butter and cut it in with a pastry blender until there are no pieces larger than a pea.
2. Stir in buttermilk adding just enough to moisten all flour. Do not overmix.
3. Stick the bowl in the fridge while preheat the air fryer.
4. Preheat air fryer to 400°F/200°C.
5. Place a piece of parchment paper in the air fryer basket, spray it with cooking spray and use a greased 1/4 cup measuring cup to scoop dough and drop it on the parchment paper. cook about 5 biscuits at a time. Lightly spray tops of biscuits with oil.
6. Air fry for 9 minutes. Brush tops with melted butter.
7. Repeat with second batch of biscuits.

Calories: 226kcal | Carbohydrates: 32g | Protein: 5g | Fat: 18g | Sodium: 218mg | Fiber: 1g | Sugar: 3g

AIR FRIED OREOS

Serving Size	Prep Time	Cooking time	Total Time
8 Servings	5 Minutes	5 Minutes	10 Minutes

Ingredients

- 8 Oreos
- 1 can crescent rolls
- Powdered sugar for dusting, optional

Directions

1. Separate crescent rolls and spread out on a baking sheet or plate.
2. Place one Oreo in each crescent roll. Gently wrap the dough around the cookie and place into air fryer basket.
3. Air fry at 350°F/180°C for 5 minutes.
4. Remove fried Oreos from basket and dust with powdered sugar while warm. Serve immediately.

Calories: 155kcal | Carbohydrates: 20g | Protein: 2g | Fat: 8g | fiber 1g. Sugar: 3g

SWEET APPLES

Serving Size	Prep Time	Cooking time	Total Time
4 Servings	10 Minutes	7 Minutes	17 Minutes

Ingredients

- 6 apples cored and diced
- 50g brown sugar
- 50g white sugar
- ¼ tsp ground cloves
- ¼ tsp pumpkin pie spice
- ½ tsp ground cinnamon
- 60g water

Directions

1. Place all ingredients in an oven-safe bowl and mix to coat the apples with seasonings and water. Place bowl into air fryer basket.
2. Air fry the apple mixture at 350°F/180°C for 6 minutes. Stir apples and cook for 2 minutes. Serve warm.

Calories: 253kcal | Carbohydrates: 66g | Protein: 1g | Fat: 11g | Sodium:8mg | Fiber: 7g | Sugar: 56g

CREAMED CORN CASSEROLE

Serving Size	Prep Time	Cooking time	Total Time
6 Servings	5 Minutes	45 Minutes	50 Minutes

Ingredients

- 125g butter melted
- 80g All Purpose flour
- 70g sugar
- 2 eggs beaten
- 120g milk
- 1 can corn drained
- 1 can creamed corn

Directions

1. In a medium sized bowl, add flour and butter. Whisk until smooth.
2. Add in milk, beaten eggs and sugar. Whisk to combine.
3. Add in drained whole kernal corn and creamed corn. Stir to combine.
4. Pour the mixture into an oven safe bowl. Put into air fryer basket. Cook at 350°F/180°C for 45 minutes.
5. Let rest for 10 minutes, then serve.

Calories: 365kcal | Carbohydrates: 64g | Protein: 7g | Fat: 16g | fiber 1g. Sugar: 18g

PUMPKIN PIE

Serving Size	Prep Time	Cooking time	Total Time
8 Servings	5 Minutes	45 Minutes	50 Minutes

Ingredients

- 450g pumpkin puree
- 120ml full fat coconut milk
- 3 eggs
- ⅛ tsp all spice
- 1 tbsp pumpkin pie spice
- ¼ tsp salt
- 120ml maple syrup
- 1 pre-made pie shell

Directions

1. Whisk together all ingredients until smooth. (except pie crust).
2. Pour the pumpkin pie mixture into the pre-made shell.
3. Air Fry 3250°F/163°C for 25 minutes. Then lower the temperature to to 300°F/150°C for 20 minutes until set in the middle.
4. Let cool for 20 minutes, then cool in the refrigerator for at least 2 hours.

Calories: 126kcal | Carbohydrates: 19g | Protein: 3g | Fat: 15g | Sodium:103mg | Fiber: 2g | Sugar: 14g

CORN BREAD

Serving Size	Prep Time	Cooking time	Total Time
8 Servings	5 Minutes	30 Minutes	35 Minutes

Ingredients

- 160g cornmeal
- 125g plain flour
- 140g sugar
- 1 tsp salt
- 1 tbsp baking powder
- 1 large egg
- 250g creamed corn
- 80ml oil

Directions

1. In a large mixing bowl, add cornmeal, flour, sugar, salt, baking powder. Mix, Then add egg, creamed corn, and oil. Mix until combined.
2. Grease a 20×20 cm square baking pan with cooking spray. Pour corn bread mixture into the greased pan.
3. Put pan in the air fryer. Air Fry at 180°C for 30 minutes. Insert a toothpick in center of corn bread and when it comes out clean, it's done. If not, leave corn bread in the air fryer for 10 minutes.
4. Remove from air fryer. Allow to cool in the pan. Serve.

calories: 415kcal, carbohydrates: 66g, protein: 7g, fat: 15g, fiber: 4g, sugar: 24g.

PEACH CRISP

Serving Size	Prep Time	Cooking time	Total Time
6 Servings	10 Minutes	20 Minutes	30 Minutes

Ingredients

- 5 peaches, (pitted, peeled, & cut into 0.5cm slices)
- 2 tbsp brown sugar
- 1 tbsp cornstarch
- 1 tsp vanilla extract
- For the topping
- 60g plain flour
- 50g old-fashioned rolled oats
- 160g granulated sugar
- 1/2 tsp cinnamon
- 1/4 tsp salt
- 60g softened unsalted butter, (cut into cubes)

Directions

1. Preheat air fryer at 350°F/175°C. Grease a baking dish that will fit in the air fryer basket.
2. In a large mixing bowl, add peach slices, brown sugar, cornstarch and vanilla. Mix until all combined. Transfer peach slices into the prepared baking dish.
3. In the same bowl, add flour, oats, sugar, cinnamon, salt and butter. Mix with hands until crumbly. Sprinkle topping mixture over the peaches.
4. Air Fry at for 20 minutes until golden.
5. Remove from air fryer and set aside for 5 minutes. Serve with ice cream.

calories: 250kcal, carbohydrates: 33g, protein: 4g, fat: 11g, sugar: 22g.

MINI LEMON PIES

Serving Size	Prep Time	Cooking time	Total Time
12 Servings	20 Minutes	6 Minutes	26 Minutes

Ingredients

- 2 eggs
- Juice & zest of 1 lemon
- 40g plain flour
- 60g melted butter
- 200g sweetened condensed milk
- 125ml milk

Directions

1. Grease and flour silicone mini muffin tins.
2. In a large mixing bowl, whisk all the ingredients until combined.
3. Divide the batter into prepared muffin tins.
4. Put muffin tins in the air fryer basket.
5. Air fry for 6 mins at 320°F/160°C. Repeat with the remaining pies.
6. Remove from air fryer, Let pies cool for 5 mins. Then serve.

117kcal, Fat: 6.5g, Carbohydrates: 12g, Protein:3g

PEANUT BUTTER OAT COOKIES

Serving Size	Prep Time	Cooking time	Total Time
12 Servings	15 Minutes	15 Minutes	30 Minutes

Ingredients

- 110g porridge oats
- 50g smooth salted peanut butter
- 200g unsweetened apple puree
- 35g dried cranberries
- 25g dark chocolate chips

Directions

1. Line the air fryer basket with baking paper
2. In a large mixing bowl, mix all the ingredients until a dough is formed
3. Divide the dough into 6 balls, pressing down to flatten (1cm thick).
4. Put 3 cookies in the fryer basket
5. bake for 12 mins at 180c. Repeat with the other 3 cookies.
6. Let cookies cool for 5 mins. Then serve.

170kcal, Fat: 7g, Carbohydrates: 21g, Protein:6g

CHOCOLATE CHIP COOKIES

Serving Size	Prep Time	Cooking time	Total Time
40 Servings	3 Minutes	7 Minutes	10 Minutes

Ingredients

- 180g unsalted butter softened
- 200g sugar
- 60g brown sugar
- 2 large eggs
- 1 tsp vanilla
- 250g plain flour
- ½ tsp salt
- ½ tsp baking soda
- 340g chocolate chips

Directions

1. In a large mixing bowl, add butter, sugar, and brown sugar. Whisk butter and sugars until smooth & creamy.
2. Add eggs, vanilla, salt, baking soda, and flour. Mix until cookie dough is thick and creamy. Add in the chocolate chips, mix until they combined.
3. Line the air fryer basket with parchment paper.
4. Use a cookie scoop to shape the cookie dough into balls. Put the cookie balls in air fryer basket.
5. Air Fry at 300°F/150°C for 7 minutes until golden brown, let them sit in the basket for an additional 2 minutes before transferring to cooking rack.

Calories: 130kcal, Carbohydrates: 17g, Protein: 1.7g, Fat: 6.5g, Fiber: 1g, Sugar: 11g

EGGY BREAD

Serving Size	Prep Time	Cooking time	Total Time
4 Servings	5 Minutes	5 Minutes	10 Minutes

Ingredients

- 225ml heavy cream
- 1 egg beaten
- 30g powdered sugar
- 1 tsp cinnamon
- 8 slices bread

Directions

1. Preheat air fryer to 400°F/205°C with basket inside.
2. Toast bread in batches for 4 mins.
3. In a large mixing bowl, mix together remaining ingredients.
4. Once toasted, dip toast into mixture, covering both sides.
5. In batches, air fry for 5 mins, flipping halfway through cooking time.
6. Serve with fruit and sugar or syrup.

342kcal, Fat: 18g, Carbohydrates: 20g, Protein: 13g

AIR FRIED CHURROS

Serving Size	Prep Time	Cooking time	Total Time
8 Servings	8 Minutes	12 Minutes	20 Minutes

Ingredients

- 225ml water
- 80g unsalted butter, (cut into cubes)
- 2 tbsp sugar
- Pinch of salt
- 125g plain flour
- 2 large eggs
- 1 tsp vanilla extract
- Cooking spray
- Coating:
- 100g granulated sugar
- 1 tsp ground cinnamon

Directions

1. In a medium saucepan over medium heat, add water, butter, sugar, and salt. Once boiled, reduce heat.
2. Add flour to the water/butter mixture. Stir constantly and cook until the dough is smooth. Transfer into a mixing bowl, set aside for 5 minutes.
3. Add eggs and vanilla extract to dough and mix until dough comes together. Transfer to a large piping bag fitted with a large star-shaped tip.
4. Pipe churros to greased baking sheet, into 10cm lengths. Refrigerate for 1 hour.
5. Put churros in Air Fryer basket, leaving about 1cm space. Spray with cooking spray.
6. Air Fry at 370°F/190°C for 12 minutes.
7. In a shallow plate, add sugar and cinnamon. Mix and toss churros in them to coat.

calories: 204kcal, carbohydrates: 27g, protein: 3g, fat: 9g, fsugar: 15g.

APPLE CRUMBLE

Serving Size	Prep Time	Cooking time	Total Time
4 Servings	10 Minutes	20 Minutes	30 Minutes

Ingredients

- 120g plain flour
- 100g white sugar
- 60g cold salted butter, cubed
- ½ tsp ground cinnamon
- ½ tsp baking powder
- ¼ tsp ground nutmeg
- cooking spray
- 150g apples, (peeled, cored, & diced)

Directions

1. Preheat air fryer to 347°F/175°C.
2. In a large mixing bowl, add flour, sugar, and butter. Mix by hands until crumbly. Add cinnamon, baking powder, and nutmeg. Mix.
3. Spray 4 ramekins with cooking spray. Add crumble to the bottom of ramekins; top with some apples. Repeat 2 times, ending with crumble on top.
4. Cover the ramekins with foil.
5. Air fry for 20 minutes until apples are tender. Remove foil and air fry for 3 minutes until crumble is golden brown.

350 calories; protein 3.5g; carbohydrates 60g; fat 12g; sugar: 33g.

APPLE FRITTERS

Serving Size	Prep Time	Cooking time	Total Time
10 Servings	15 Minutes	15 Minutes	35 Minutes

Ingredients

- 100g sugar
- 1/2 tsp ground cinnamon
- 1 apple (chopped & peeled)
- 5 Buttermilk Biscuits dough
- 3 tbsp melted butter

Directions

1. In small mixing bowl, mix sugar and cinnamon. In another bowl, mix chopped apple and 2 tbsp of the cinnamon/sugar mixture until combined.
2. Separate each biscuit dough into 2 layers. Press each into 10cm round. Spoon 2 tbsp of the apples into center of each round. Fold edges over filling; pinch to seal. Brush biscuits with melted butter.
3. Put 5 of the biscuits on parchment in air fryer basket. Spray with cooking spray. (you may need to work in batches)
4. Air fry at 320°F/160°C for 15 minutes, flipping halfway through cooking time.
5. When time is up, remove biscuits from air fryer, brush biscuits with butter and roll in sugar or cinnamon/sugar until well coated

Calories: 170kcal | Carbohydrates: 25g | Protein: 1g | Fat: 7g | Sugar: 13g

CHOCOLATE FUDGE BROWNIES

Serving Size	Prep Time	Cooking time	Total Time
10 Servings	15 Minutes	25 Minutes	40 Minutes

Ingredients

- 250g butter, (melted)
- 200g semisweet chocolate chips, (melted)
- 75g unsweetened cocoa powder
- 200g sugar
- 50g brown sugar
- 1 tbsp vanilla
- 1/2 tsp salt
- 4 eggs
- 150g plain flour

Directions

1. In a large mixing bowl, add melted butter and melted chocolate chips. Mix until combined.
2. Add in the unsweetened cocoa powder, and the sugar. Mix until combined
3. Add the remaining the ingredients in. Mix.
4. Spread the batter into an air fryer safe pan.
5. Air fry at 320°F/160°C for 20-25 minutes.
6. Remove from air fryer, let cool before serving.

Calories: 450kcal | Carbohydrates: 53g | Protein: 5.5g | Fat: 28g | Fiber: 4.5g | Sugar: 35g

STRAWBERRY RHUBARB CRUMBLES

Serving Size	Prep Time	Cooking time	Total Time
5 Servings	7 Minutes	18 Minutes	25 Minutes

Ingredients

- 450g strawberries, (hulled & halved)
- 450g rhubarb, trimmed & cut into 1.5cm pieces
- 50g + 3 tbsp sugar, divided
- 1 tbsp cornstarch
- 6 tbsp unsalted butter, cut into small cubes
- 100g plain flour
- ¼ tsp salt
- 30g almonds, chopped
- Cooking spray

Directions

1. Preheat the air fryer to 350°F/175°C. Spray small ramekins with cooking spray and set aside.
2. In a large mixing bowl, add strawberries, rhubarb, 50g sugar and cornstarch. Mix.
3. In another bowl, add the butter and flour, rubbing together with hands until they resemble breadcrumbs. Then, add 3 tbsp sugar, salt & almonds and mix the mixture together.
4. Divide the fruit mixture among the ramekins and top with the crumble mixture. Put in the air fryer and air fry for 18 minutes.

280kcal | Carbohydrates: 38g | Protein: 4g | Fat: 14g | Fiber: 4g | Sugar: 18g

APPLE PIE FILO PASTRIES

Serving Size	Prep Time	Cooking time	Total Time
10 Servings	24 Minutes	6 Minutes	30 Minutes

Ingredients

- 3 apples, (finely sliced & chopped)
- 1 tbsp lemon juice
- 2 tsp plain flour
- 2 tsp cinnamon
- 2 tsp brown sugar
- 1/2 tsp nutmeg
- 1/2 tsp ground cloves
- 10 sheets filo pastry
- 170g butter, (melted)

Directions

1. In a large mixing bowl, add apples, lemon juice, flour, sugar & spices. Mix.
2. Keep the pastry covered with a damp tea towel while you work.
3. Put one of filo sheet on a large piece of parchment paper, brush with butter.
4. Put 6 tbsp of apple filling in the middle of the filo. Roll up the sheet stopping once or twice to brush the pastry with butter. Once done, brush up and down, with butter. repeat with remaining filo pastry.
5. Air fry at 320°F/160°C for 6 minutes.
6. Remove from air fryer. Allow to cool slightly before serving.

Calories: 219kcal | Carbohydrates: 20g | Protein: 2g | Fat: 15g | Fiber: 2g | Sugar: 7g

CHOCOLATE CUPCAKES

Serving Size	Prep Time	Cooking time	Total Time
10 Servings	20 Minutes	12 Minutes	32 Minutes

Ingredients

- 100g unsweetened cocoa powder
- 125ml hot water
- 200g sugar
- 70ml vegetable oil
- 125ml milk
- 1 egg
- 1 tsp vanilla extract
- 120g flour
- 3/4 tsp baking powder
- 3/4 tsp baking soda
- 1/2 tsp salt

Chocolate Buttercream

- 8 tbsp butter, (softened)
- 225g powdered sugar
- 3 tbsp cocoa powder
- Pinch of salt
- 1/4 tsp vanilla extract
- 1 to 4 tbsp milk

Directions

1. Preheat the air fryer to 311°F/155°C.
2. Line 12 silicone cupcake holders with paper cupcake liners.
3. In a large bowl, add cocoa and hot water, mix until cocoa dissolved. Add sugar, oil, milk, egg, and vanilla. Whisk. Sift in flour, baking powder, baking soda, and salt and stir.
4. Divide the batter into cupcake holders and put them in air fryer basket.
5. Air fry for 12 minutes. Remove from air fryer and let cool.

Chocolate buttercream frosting

1. Beat the butter until soft & creamy. Add powdered sugar & cocoa. Beat until combined. Add salt & vanilla extract and beat. Slowly add milk and beat.
2. Spread on cooled cupcakes.

Calories: 219kcal | Carbohydrates: 20g | Protein: 2g | Fat: 15g | Fiber: 2g | Sugar: 7g

BANANA BUNDT CAKE

Serving Size	Prep Time	Cooking time	Total Time
4 Servings	5 Minutes	15 Minutes	20 Minutes

Ingredients

For the cake

- 2 bananas
- 1 egg
- 150g sugar
- 70ml oil
- 1 tsp vanilla extract
- 120g plain flour
- 1/2 tsp cinnamon
- 1 tsp baking powder
- 1/2 tsp baking soda
- 1/2 tsp salt

Cream cheese icing

- 2 tbsp butter, softened
- 60g cream cheese softened
- 100g powdered sugar
- 1 tsp vanilla extract
- 2 tbsp heavy cream

Directions

For the cake:

1. In a large bowl, mash bananas, then add egg. Mix. Add sugar, oil, and vanilla and mix until combined.
2. Sift in dry ingredients over banana/egg mixture. Fold dry ingredients into the batter. Pour the batter into a mini bundt pan. Add into air fryer basket.
3. Air fry at 320°F/160°C for 14 minutes.
4. Rotate 180° and air fry for another 15 minutes.
5. Remove from air fryer. Let the cake cool completely.

For the icing:

1. Microwave butter & cream cheese for 7 to 10 seconds then stir and microwave for another 7 seconds.
2. Add the powdered sugar and vanilla. Stir until smooth. Whisk in the cream.
3. Drizzle the icing over the cake and serve.

Calories: 219kcal | Carbohydrates: 20g | Protein: 2g | Fat: 15g | Fiber: 2g | Sugar: 7g

CINNAMON ROLLS

Serving Size	Prep Time	Cooking time	Total Time
6 Servings	15 Minutes	15 Minutes	30 Minutes

Ingredients

For the rolls
- 120g plain flour
- 4 tsp granulated sugar
- 1 tsp baking powder
- 1/8 tsp baking soda
- 1/4 tsp salt
- 4 tbsp cold butter, cut into cubes
- 80ml whole milk

For the cinnamon filling
- 2 tbsp melted butter
- 1/2 cup brown sugar
- 1 tsp ground cinnamon

Cream Cheese Icing
- 4 tbsp cream cheese, softened
- 1 tbsp butter, softened
- 60g powdered sugar
- 1/4 tsp vanilla extract
- 1 tsp milk (optional)

Directions

1. Preheat the air fryer to 320°F/160°C. Grease a 10-cm round cake pan.
2. In a large bowl, add flour, sugar, baking powder, baking soda, and salt. Mix. Add butter and smash it into the flour until it looks like sand.
3. Add in milk. Mix until form a dough. Transfer dough to floured surface and roll out into a 23cm x 30cm rectangle.
4. Mix the cinnamon ingredients filling in a bowl. Spread the filling over the dough. Roll dough up into a log.
5. Cut the log into 6 pieces and place them into the cake pan.
6. Put the pan into the air fryer basket and air fry for 14 minutes.
7. In a large bowl, add cream cheese and butter and stir well. Add the powdered sugar, vanilla and mix until creamy. Add in the milk.
8. Remove rolls from air fryer and drizzle the glaze over the top.

CALORIES: 341, FAT: 17g, CARBOHYDRATES: 45g, FIBER: 1g, SUGAR: 28g, PROTEIN: 3g

STRAWBERRY SHORTCAKE

Serving Size	Prep Time	Cooking time	Total Time
6 Servings	5 Minutes	15 Minutes	20 Minutes

Ingredients

- 250g strawberries, (sliced)
- 4 tbsp. granulated sugar
- 250g all-purpose flour
- 3 tbsp. butter cold, cubed
- 1 tsp baking powder
- ¼ tsp baking soda
- pinch salt
- 125ml buttermilk
- Garnish: whipped cream
- Cooking spray

Directions

1. Preheat air fryer at 300°F/150°C.
2. In a large mixing bowl, mix the strawberries with 2 tbsp. sugar, and set aside, and stir occasionally.
3. In another mixing bowl, mix flour baking soda, baking powder, 2 tbsp. sugar and salt. Add butter and mash it into the flour mixture until combined.
4. Add in buttermilk and mix until to form a sticky dough.
5. Put the dough into a baking dish, spread in an even layer. Place into air fryer basket and air fry for 15 minutes or until golden.
6. When time is up, remove from air fryer, allow to cool, serve with strawberries over the top and garnish with whipped cream.

Calories: 244kcal Carbohydrates: 31gProtein: 5gFat: 12gFiber: 2gSugar: 7g

BANANA SOUFFLE

Serving Size	Prep Time	Cooking time	Total Time
6 Servings	15 Minutes	15 Minutes	30 Minutes

Ingredients

- 2 medium ripe bananas
- 2 large eggs
- ½ tsp. cinnamon
- Cooking spray

Directions

1. In a blender, put the banana, eggs and cinnamon and blend until smooth.
2. Spray ramekins with cooking spray.
3. Divide the souffle batter into the ramekins & place them in the air fryer basket.
4. Air fry at 350°F / 180°C for 15 min.
5. When tome is up, remove. Serve immediately.

Calories: 85kcal | Carbohydrates: 14g | Protein: 3g | Fat: 2g | Fiber: 2g | Sugar: 7g

BANANA BREAD

Serving Size	Prep Time	Cooking time	Total Time
8 Servings	40 Minutes	30 Minutes	40 Minutes

Ingredients

- 90g plain flour
- 1 tsp ground cinnamon
- 1/2 tsp salt
- 1/4 tsp baking soda
- 2 bananas, (mashed)
- 2 large eggs, (beaten)
- 100g white sugar
- 60ml whole milk
- 2 tbsp oil
- 1/2 tsp vanilla extract
- 5 tbsp walnuts, (chopped)
- Cooking spray

Directions

1. Preheat air fryer to 311°F / 155°C. Spray a 15-cm round cake pan with cooking spray.
2. In a large mixing bowl, add flour, cinnamon, salt, and baking soda. Whisk together.
3. In a medium mixing bowl, add banana, eggs, sugar, milk, oil, walnuts, and vanilla extract. Mix until combined.
4. Add banana mixture to the flour mixture. Mix until batter is combined. Transfer into prepared cake pan.
5. Put pan in air fryer basket. Air fry for 30 minutes, until a toothpick comes out clean when inserted in the middle.
6. Remove from air fryer, transfer into wire rack to cool for 15 minutes. Remove from pan, serve.

Per Serving: Calories: 198kcal | Carbohydrates: 29g | Protein: 4.5g | Fat: 8g | Fiber: 2g | Sugar: 17g

BLUEBERRY SCONES

Serving Size	Prep Time	Cooking time	Total Time
16 Servings	10 Minutes	6 Minutes	16 Minutes

Ingredients

- 180g butter slightly softened
- 250g plain flour
- 50g sugar
- 2 tsp baking powder
- 1 large egg
- 140g fresh or frozen blueberries
- 4 tbsp milk

Directions

1. In a medium mixing bowl, add butter, flour, sugar, and baking powder. mix until it become crumbly.
2. Add in the egg, milk, one tbsp at a time, until the dough forms. Stir in the blueberries.
3. Roll the dough, until it is 1.5cm thick. Cut with 5cm cutter into rounds.
4. Spray air fryer basket with cooking spray.
5. Put scones in air fryer basket in a single layer.
6. Cook at 380°F/195°C for 5-6 minutes, until golden.

Calories: 101kcal, Carbohydrates: 20g, Protein: 3g, Fat: 1g, Fiber: 1g Sugar: 6g

AIR FRYER DONUTS

Serving Size	Prep Time	Cooking time	Total Time
8 Servings	20 Minutes	5 Minutes	25 Minutes

Ingredients

- 450g tube jumbo biscuits divided
- 20g melted butter
- 100g sugar
- 1 tbsp. ground cinnamon
- 60g powdered sugar

Directions

1. Preheat air fryer at 360°F/180°C for 5 minutes.
2. Cut out each biscuit center, set the centers aside.
3. Put 4 biscuits in the air fryer basket (not touching each other sides). Air fry for 6 minutes, flipping halfway through cooking time. (you may need to work in patches)
4. In a large mixing bowl, put powdered sugar. In another mixing bowl, put cinnamon and sugar, and mix until combined.
5. When time is up, remove donuts from air fryer, coat donuts in butter and roll in sugar or cinnamon/sugar until well coated.
6. Put donuts holes in the air fryer basket. Air fry for 3 minutes, flipping halfway through cooking time.
7. When time is up, remove donuts holes from air fryer, coat in butter and roll in sugar or cinnamon/sugar until well coated.

Calories: 360kcal | Carbohydrates: 49g | Protein: 4g | Fat: 21g | Fiber: 1g | Sugar: 14g |

HAND PIES

Serving Size	Prep Time	Cooking time	Total Time
7 Servings	15 Minutes	7 Minutes	22 Minutes

Ingredients

- 420g refrigerated pie crusts or homemade - two crusts
- 450g fresh or frozen fruit (apples, peaches, blueberries, strawberries, etc.)
- 2 tbsp lemon juice
- 170g water or juice
- 30g unsalted butter
- 50g brown sugar
- ¼ tsp salt
- 14g cornstarch
- 30g water

Directions

1. Cut each pie crusts into seven, 3.5"/9cm circles (14 small crusts total).
2. Prepare your apples by chopping into small cubes.
3. Place fruit and butter in a large saucepan over medium-high heat until the butter is melted and bubbling.
4. Add in your water (or juice), sugar, lemon juice, and salt and mix until combined. Bring to a simmer.
5. Combine cornstarch with water and whisk. Pour into simmering mixture and mix for 2 minutes.
6. Remove from heat and let mixture cool. place 2 tbsp of pie filling in each pie crust circle. Seal top and bottom crusts together with water and then close with a fork. Spread an egg wash over the top. Air fry at 350F/176C for 6-8 minutes.

Calories: 113kcal | Carbohydrates: 19g | Protein: 1g | Fat: 4g | Sodium: 96mg | Fiber: 2g | Sugar: 15g

PUMPKIN CHOCOLATE CHIP MUFFINS

Serving Size	Prep Time	Cooking time	Total Time
24 Servings	20 Minutes	15 Minutes	35 Minutes

Ingredients

- 3 large eggs
- 425g pumpkin puree
- 120g oil
- 125g no-sugar added applesauce
- 200 g granulated sugar
- 320g all-purpose flour
- 2 tsp pumpkin pie spice
- 1 tsp baking soda
- ½ tsp baking powder
- ½ tsp salt
- Chocolate chips to taste

Directions

1. In a large bowl, whisk wet ingredients. eggs, pumpkin, oil, applesauce and sugar.
2. In a separate bowl, stir dry ingredients. flour, pumpkin pie spice, baking soda, baking powder and salt.
3. Add dry ingredients to wet ingredients. Mix until combined and add in the chocolate chips to taste (don't overmix).
4. Place up to 9 silicone muffin liners in the air fryer basket. Lightly spray with cooking spray. Add batter to the liners, about ¾ way full.
5. air fry at 330°F/165°C for 15 minutes.
6. remove from air fryer. Let cool slightly then remove from the liner.
7. Repeat with the remaining batter.

Calories: 186kcal | Carbohydrates: 27g | Protein: 2g | Fat: 8g | Sodium: 116mg | Fiber: 1g | Sugar: 15g

LEMON BAKED DONUTS

Serving Size	Prep Time	Cooking time	Total Time
8 Servings	15 Minutes	10 Minutes	25 Minutes

Ingredients

- 40g lemon juice and 2 tsp lemon zest
- 3 large eggs
- 420g can sweetened condensed milk
- 150g self rising flour

Lemon Glaze

- 1 tbsp lemon juice 1 medium lemon or bottled
- 130g powdered sugar
- milk as needed

Directions

1. Preheat the air fryer at 330°F/165°C.
2. In a small bowl, combine lemon juice, lemon zest, eggs, and sweetened condensed milk together. add flour and mix until completely incorporated.
3. Spray silicone donut molds with cooking spray. Pour batter into molds.
4. air fry for 9 minutes. Let cool in the mold, then remove from the mold and let cool completely.
5. Beat lemon juice with powdered sugar. Add any milk until the glaze reaches desired consistency.
6. Once cooled, drizzle or dip glaze on top of donuts.

Calories: 211kcal | Carbohydrates: 38g | Protein: 6g | Fat: 4g | Sodium: 60mg | Fiber: 1g | Sugar: 28g

NUTELLA FRENCH TOAST ROLL UP

Serving Size	Prep Time	Cooking time	Total Time
5 Servings	14 Minutes	6 Minutes	50 Minutes

Ingredients

- 10 slices bread
- 3 large eggs
- 2 tbsp milk
- 4 tbsp white sugar
- 1 tsp cinnamon
- 70g Nutella, 1 tsp per slice of bread

Directions

1. Dry out the bread the air fryer by placing the bread in the air fryer for 2 minutes at 350°F/177°C.
2. Whisk eggs and milk together in a shallow bowl. Set aside. In a separate shallow bowl, mix cinnamon and sugar. Set aside. Line air fryer basket with a piece of parchment paper and lightly spray it with cooking spray.
3. Cut off the crust on slices of bread. Flatten bread slices with rolling pin.
4. Spread a tsp Nutella on one end of bread. Roll bread in a log and dab a little Nutella on ends to help keep secure during baking.
5. Dip bread rolls in egg/milk mixture then in cinnamon/sugar mixture.
6. Place toast rolls in air fryer basket. Cook at 360°F/182°C for 6 minutes, flipping halfway through.

Calories: 319kcal | Carbohydrates: 46g | Protein: 11g | Fat: 10g | Sodium: 316mg | Fiber: 3g | Sugar: 21g

CREME BRULEE

Serving Size	Prep Time	Cooking time	Total Time
5 Servings	20 Minutes	32 Minutes	1 hour 52 minutes

Ingredients

- 6 egg yolks
- 6 tbsp sugar divided- 4 tbsp for custard, 2 tbsp for carmelizing
- 220g heavy whipping cream
- 2 tsps vanilla extract
- 1 pinch salt

Directions

1. Whisk egg yolks, 4 tbsp of sugar and salt. Add whipping cream and vanilla and whisk until blended.
2. Divide mixture evenly between 5-6 ramekins. Cover each tightly with foil. (use tinfoil wrapped all the way around the ramekin.)
3. Place in air fryer and cook at 370°F/188°C for 32 minutes.
4. remove hot ramekins and set on a rack to cool.
5. Once completely cooled, cover with plastic wrap and chill for 1 hour or up to 2 days.
6. When ready to serve, top each ramekin with 1 tsp sugar and then broil for 2-3 minutes in oven to caramelize sugar.
7. Let stand for a few mins before serving.

Calories: 567kcal | Carbohydrates: 23g | Protein: 8g | Fat: 50g | Sodium: 55mg | Sugar: 22g

SWEET POTATO PIE

Serving Size	Prep Time	Cooking time	Total Time
12 Servings	5 Minutes	15 Minutes	20 Minutes

Ingredients

Filling

- 220g cooked sweet potato puree
- 100g brown sugar
- 125g vegetable oil
- 125g heavy cream
- 2 eggs
- 1 tsp vanilla extract
- 2 tsp cinnamon
- ¼ tsp ginger
- ¼ tsp nutmeg
- pinch of cloves

Crust

- pre-made pie crust

Directions

1. Preheat the air fryer to 300°F/180°C.
2. Press the pie dough into the bottom of several 3-inch/8-cm pie plates.
3. Place all of the filling ingredients in a bowl and mix until smooth and silky.
4. Divide the the filling among the pie plates and place them in the air fryer basket.
5. Bake for 15 minutes until pies are set and cooked through.

Calories: 181kcal, Carbohydrates: 14g, Protein: 2g, Fat: 14g, Fiber: 1g, Sugar: 11g.